This item may be recalled before the date stamped below.
You must return it when it is recalled or you will be fined.

NORMAL LOAN

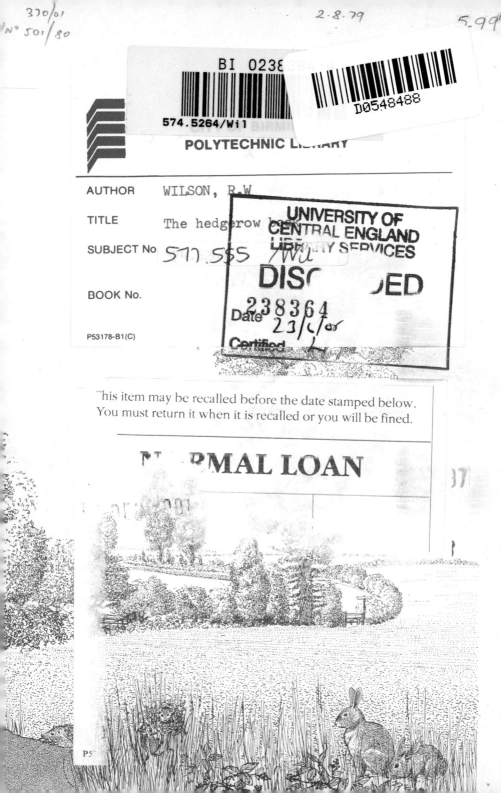

The Hedgerow Book

The Hedgerow Book

Ron Wilson

DAVID & CHARLES
Newton Abbot London North Pomfret (Vt)

Drawings by Denys Baker

British Library Cataloguing in Publication Data
Wilson, Ron
    The hedgerow book.
    1. Windbreaks, shelterbelts, etc.—Great Britain
    I. Title
    574.5'264   SD409.5

    ISBN 0 7153 7728 0

Typeset by Ronset Limited, Darwen, Lancashire
and printed in Great Britain
by Biddles Limited, Guildford
for David & Charles (Publishers) Limited
Brunel House   Newton Abbot   Devon

Published in the United States of America
by David & Charles Inc
North Pomfret   Vermont 05053   USA

Contents

Acknowledgements

A number of people have helped in preparing this book. I would like to thank Don Wright for the many hours which he spent reading the manuscript, and Emma Wood, who edited most of it and who persuaded me to continue when things got tough! The typing has been undertaken by Mrs J. Hurley and Mrs L. Reynolds, and I am grateful to them for deciphering the many scribbled notes on the manuscript. Finally I would like to thank Dr Max Hooper, who has given me permission to quote his famous hedgerow dating system.

Introduction

Viewed from an aeroplane high above, the British countryside looks like a gigantic random patchwork quilt. No two patches appear to be of equal shape and size. In some parts, like the Fenland region of eastern England, the patches are large; in other areas, including parts of the Midlands and the south-west, they are relatively small. The mosaic effect of the fields is enhanced and highlighted by the wide variety of hedges that mark their boundaries. Some of these have been deliberately planted; others have grown up accidentally.

But how much do we know about these integral features of the landscape? What do we know of their place in the ecological pattern? Are they as important to wildlife as conservationists maintain? Is their importance affected by their management? How do we know what effect they have on the farmer's land, and the crops he grows there? How old are they? Although many hedges have been studied in detail, we still have much to learn.

The *Concise Oxford Dictionary* defines a hedge as a 'Fence of bushes or low trees'. But even a cursory glance will show that no two hedges are identical, even if they contain the same mixture of shrubs and herbs. Their height and thickness will differ, according to age, soil and situation, cutting and general management.

While carrying out intensive studies of hedgerows, Dr Max Hooper and his colleagues came to the general conclusion that they could be placed in one of seven categories. In the *remnant hedge*, only a few of the shrubs remain, and it is of no practical use to the farmer. There are

7

Here is a mixture of old field systems with newer, more regular and therefore more easily managed fields. The area about one-third of the way up has lost many of its trees and some of its hedges, in contrast to the foreground and upper two-thirds. The single trees, together with the hedges, act as links between the smaller areas of spinneys and copses (*Aerofilms*)

various ways of managing hedges, but the usual, and most efficient, method, when practised properly, is that used for the *laid hedge*, in which man has produced an effective stockproof barrier. *Mechanically pollarded hedges* owe their form to a mechanical cutter, which has lopped off the larger branches. *Clipped hedges* take on a triangular outline, particularly on the roadside face. *Overgrown hedges*, common where no management has been undertaken for years, are no use for keeping in stock, unless a second man-made barrier of stakes and wire fills in the gaps. Cattle have removed the vegetation and left large gaps at the base of the hedge, allowing the shrubs to grow upwards, unchecked, without proper branching low down.

Certain species of hedges do well without being clipped regularly, and there are *unclipped boundary hedges* which are impenetrable by stock. The final type, which could be called *spread hedges*, includes those where the bottom of the hedge has been allowed to grow outwards through lack of management, either by hand or cutter. In this case some shrubs, particularly hawthorn and blackthorn, have spread into both the field and the verge.

The Changing Landscape

People driving through the eastern counties of Britain during the 1970s will get a different impression from that gained by William Marshall as he travelled through Norfolk in the late 1700s. Describing his journey in his book *The Rural Economy of Norfolk*, published in 1787, he found 'hedges high and full of trees', and he felt that he was 'ever on the verge of a forest'. Norfolk is certainly one of those counties which demonstrate the change which has taken place over the years as not only hedgerows, but also the accompanying ditches, banks and trees, have been removed. Aesthetically the landscape here is much less interesting than in, for example, parts of the Midlands and south-west. The effects of these changes on wildlife are less obvious.

In some parts of the country, hedgerows as a 'normal' feature of the landscape are rapidly disappearing. The rate of hedgerow removal varies from one region to another—the estimate of its speed varies greatly according to the references consulted!

Unfortunately we do not know how much hedgerow there was before the modern uprooting campaign began. In counties with only a small total length of hedges, any removals may be a drastic loss, both aesthetically and for wildlife.

Various estimates have been made of the length of Britain's hedgerows, but the results are not too reliable. One researcher's over-estimate of the total length of field boundaries in the mid-1950s was

The seemingly endless traditional quilt of fields seamed by hedgerows—now under threat

based on two obviously wrong assumptions. Firstly, he decided that a field of 5 acres (2 hectares) in extent had a hedge all the way round; yet most fields share at least one hedge with the next field. A field surrounded by four others would not have any hedges! This obviously reduces the length considerably. Secondly, this researcher assumed that all fields were regular and of uniform size: the merest glance at the aerial photographs in this book shows that the field system is made up of irregularly shaped units, large, medium and small. Naturally this results in less length of hedge than if the field size was uniform. So the earlier figure of 1,700,000 miles (2,735,300 km) is probably halved, and there is no more than 750,000 miles (1,206,750 km).

In parts of the British Isles, field boundaries usually consist of such features as drystone walls, like those in the Cotswolds, Derbyshire or the Yorkshire Dales. In other areas, such as the Fens of Eastern England, there are no visible field barriers, only ditches.

To obtain accurate figures it is necessary to look at hedge removal over a wide area. The rate is different in various counties: in eastern England it is much more rapid than in the Midlands. A small survey of one parish in Northamptonshire, using aerial photography, has shown that very little hedgerow has disappeared there.

Between 1946 and 1963, it has been estimated that about 5,000 miles (over 8,000 km) of hedgerow have been removed annually, which amounts to 85,000 miles (136,790 km) for the seventeen-year period. A further survey suggests that over a twenty-four-year period it was 50,000 miles (80,467 km). It seems likely that the wholesale uprooting of these valuable wildlife habitats and aesthetically pleasing countryside features is now over. On the other hand, it is highly unlikely that any new hedges will be planted.

As man claimed land from what was originally probably forest in parts of the South-west, the fields have acquired an irregular outline, and hedges, small woods, copses and spinneys, as well as single trees, are an important feature of the landscape and a valuable asset for wildlife (*Aerofilms*)

Once again I see
These hedge-rows, hardly hedge-rows, little lines
Of sportive wood run wild . . .

William Wordsworth, *Tintern Abbey Revisited*

1

The First Hedges

In some parts of the British Isles the hedgerow has a history of at least two thousand years; in other areas it is relatively recent. When did hedges first appear on the scene? Although there was probably human life here as the Ice Age began to lose its grip, pre 1200 BC, it is only in quite recent times that patterns of agriculture began to change.

Four thousand years after the disappearance of the ice, Mesolithic people—Britain's first 'modern' man—appeared on the scene. Nomadic, lacking the wherewithal to cultivate plants, they collected edible wild berries, fruits and nuts, and hunted for meat, killing all manner of wild animals, including boar and deer, as well as taking fish from the rivers.

Then began the gradual change to an 'established' civilised way of life, the change from man the hunter and collector to man the farmer. Instead of collecting food, he now started growing it and keeping animals for himself. Close to his homestead he cleared a patch of land to grow his crops and fixed a paddock for keeping and grazing his animals. As he cleared rocks and boulders from his fields, he used them to mark his boundaries. Seeds of various species of wild plants, brought by birds and animals, would have grown up among them, and the earliest hedges probably began this way. The commonest and most easily established species would have included brambles and thorns.

Where Neolithic man lived 4,000 years ago, attempts were made to clear the forests. The number of trees removed was small, but nevertheless this activity marked the beginnings of the change in the agricultural pattern of the British Isles.

Old Hedges on High Moors

Some of the oldest hedges to survive, although we have no written records to show their ages, are those to be found on the high moors. Both Iron Age and Bronze Age man had widely scattered moorland settlements in various parts of the country, and their hedges became an established feature of the countryside. Two thousand years have rolled by since these hedges first appeared, but we can still follow their lines, indicating Iron- and Bronze-Age settlement areas, especially in some counties such as Cornwall. Here a collection of Bronze-Age coins was found in a hedge, indicating that it dated from at least as far back as this particular era.

The population of the British Isles increased slowly and only small amounts of land were cleared for crop-growing. In due course our ancestors must have realised that the high land was not particularly productive, and that the fertile regions were in the valleys. Although the actual spread of civilisation was haphazard, these first few, usually isolated, hamlets expanded, forming villages and eventually towns; land clearance for growing food moved ahead.

When the Romans invaded Britain it seems fairly certain that, with their methodical ways, they would have brought a system for dividing fields. Indeed it is likely that Roman hedges are to be found in various parts of the country, in particular around Brancaster in Norfolk.

So the first hedgerows grew up mainly accidentally during the Iron and Bronze Ages; deliberately planted hedges may have come with the Romans. The 'accidental' hedges would have increased with the advent of strip-farming, which was practised widely over many parts of the British Isles. Along the paths in between the strips, seedlings from shrubs would have fallen and taken root, and soon a small hedge would have become established.

The Dead Hedge

In some areas, many of the earlier hedges were not living features of the landscape as we know them today, but built from stakes, which were interwoven to form a barrier impenetrable by stock. What is more, unlike living hedges, they were quickly erected. One record of this type of structure survives—in an old custom observed annually at Whitby in Yorkshire. The story is that during the early part of the fourteenth century some noblemen out hunting in Eskdale wounded a wild boar. Demented with its injuries the animal fled, men and hounds in hot pursuit. Seeking refuge in a cave the boar was found by a monk from Whitby. Distressed at the sight of the wounded animal, the monk tried to protect it, and was himself attacked by the hunters.

This action would have resulted in severe penalties for the huntsmen, if the Abbot of Whitby had not intervened. He decreed that the noblemen and their successors should cut rods and stakes from a wood at Stronghold in Eskdale. Once collected the material was to be taken to the shore where a barrier—a dead hedge—had to be built. The hedge had to be strong enough to withstand the onslaught of three successive tides. Should the wrongdoers fail to perform their punishment annually, then their lands were to become the property of the Abbot of Whitby.

Originally called the *pennance hedge*, but now corrupted to the *penny hedge*, the structure is still erected each year on the shore at Whitby; stakes are sunk into the sand, thinner, more pliable branches being interwoven to form the barrier.

Assart Hedges

Where hedges are found around *assarts* (areas of farmland formed by clearance of a wood), they often contain plants that were once part of the earlier wood. The men planting the hedge would have purposely included some shrubs removed from the woodland. In earlier times, particularly during the reign of Richard I (1189–99) assarts were leased out as a source of revenue to the landowner.

The King himself made it clear to his tenants that in order to maintain his sporting activities the hedges around the fields must only be allowed to reach a maximum height of 4ft 6in (1.3m), because this was the height which deer could clear.

Hedges of History

The first actual written record of a hedge does not relate to Britain. Caesar, in his *Gallic War*, refers to a hedge which he 'found' on the border between Belgium and France. The hedge, much like the thick thorn hedges still relatively common in the Midland counties of England, was built for protection—not to keep stock in, but to keep advancing armies out. Local soldiers cut young trees, which they bent over, interweaving other growing material into them. The method is unlikely to have been the soldiers' invention and may also have been used to fence in cattle.

In Britain the first reference to a hedge is recorded in the Anglo-Saxon Chronicle. Ida of Northumberland erected a hedge in 547 when he formed a settlement called Bamburgh. This 'hedge' probably consisted of nothing more than a mound of soil. However, the word 'hedge' came originally from the Anglo-Saxon *gahaeg*, which has given its two other words, *haw* and *hay*: both have been used at times to describe a hedge. The name of the commonest hedging plant, haw-thorn, means *hedge-thorn*.

The first mention of the function and purpose of a hedge is given more than 1,200 years ago. In records dating from between 688 and 694, and known as the Laws of Ine, proposed by the King of Wessex, we find explicit instructions that the primary purpose of a hedge was to stop cattle getting in and attacking the farmer's crops. The Laws clearly indicate that it was the responsibility of the farmer to ensure that the fence around his patch was stockproof. He had no compensation if cattle managed to push through and enter his land, his only course being to drive them out.

Some of these were dead hedges. When much land remained unenclosed, the dead hedge allowed the farmer to 'move' his field. By the beginning of the seventeenth century the writer Barnaby Googe noticed that both live and dead hedges were a feature of the field boundary system.

2

Enclosure

By far the greatest amount of hedgerow has grown up as a result of the Enclosure Acts and Awards. Generally these enclosure hedges consist of a single species, such as hawthorn or blackthorn, though sometimes a number of trees and shrubs form a mixed hedge. Many hedges had a mixed start: for example, if part of a hedge was growing along the strips of a field, at the time of the enclosures other hedging species would have been planted to form a continuous field boundary.

Although, as we have seen, some of our hedges date from earlier times, the two great periods of activity were 1460 to 1600 and 1740 to 1830. During the first of these eras, many field boundaries were planted in parts of Norfolk and the Midlands. Waste land and common land, often covering extensive areas, were being divided by hedges and ditches and in some cases by walls, as sheep farming was becoming important. Some of these early hedges can still be seen. Between the thirteenth and seventeenth centuries, large amounts of land were permanently enclosed, although such action, with a few exceptions, was strictly illegal. Acts passed to prevent these enclosures did not solve the problem, as the proliferation of enclosures on the statute book bears witness.

It is difficult to discover how much land was enclosed during the fourteenth and fifteenth centuries. In some counties, where careful records were kept and have been preserved, it is possible to see that, in spite of the various Acts, land enclosure increased dramatically between the latter part of the fifteenth and the early part of the sixteenth centuries. The amount of land actually concerned was quite small, though it was not evenly distributed over the country, or for that matter any particular county: the enclosures probably had significant effects on certain communities, but little relevance for others. Most of the landowners stoutly defended their actions in enclosing land, arguing that, for example, it was beneficial to the local community: people could collect faggots for their fires from the hedges, and take stakes for fencing. When planting hedges these landowners also put in trees, which they saw as a means of providing valuable timber, often lost when woodland was chopped down.

The Great Enclosure Period

The second and most extensive period of activity was between 1740 and 1830, when innumerable Enclosure Acts and Awards were passed by parliament. Although hedgerows had been planted for many centuries, it was during this time that the English landscape was given the pattern that is familiar today.

Roadside verges also date from about the early part of the nineteenth century. Before this period various Acts were passed in an attempt to improve conditions for travellers. For example, one relating to Everdon in Northamptonshire stated that roads should be 40ft (63m) wide. This seemingly excessive width was necessary because 'mud' roads could become impassable in bad weather where hooves and wheels had beaten ruts; on a wider road, the traffic could spread out. With the coming of tarmacadam surfaces this was no longer necessary, and in some places the sides of the road were either incorporated into the field system or quietly absorbed into gardens and allotments. An interesting situation has arisen in places where a Saxon boundary hedge survives not far from a hedge dating from the time of the enclosures.

The Parliamentary Acts and Awards introduced a tidy system which in theory was relatively simple to work. Each settlement would have had six parcels of land, contained within three fields. Two of these parcels (one field) would have remained fallow. Of the remaining two fields, one would have been used for common grazing, from which hay and winter keep was also taken. The other field would have

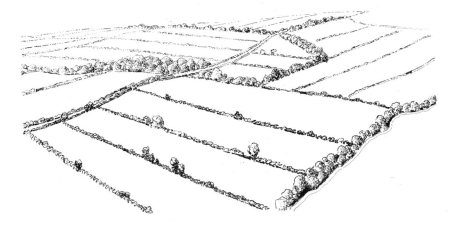

Hedges may still follow the lines established in the days of strip farming

provided land for houses, as well as small grassed areas probably used for horses. In reality, of course, it was much more difficult to put into practice, with a thousand and one local permutations.

Where the three-field system was practised, a dead hedge might be put around the grazing meadow or around the fields containing crops. Since one field bordered another, then some fields had common boundaries; and since the animals would be grazing year after year, the barrier was needed permanently. Various shrubs would seed and establish themselves along the line, and so a dead hedge would eventually become a living one.

The amount of land enclosed in various counties differed enormously. As far as can be discovered there were no Acts for Cornwall, Kent, Lancashire or Devon. Northamptonshire had the greatest percentage of land enclosed, just over half the area of the county. By contrast, in Shropshire less than one-half of one per cent was affected. In some areas, as old maps show, hedges had already appeared in the open-field system. In the 'modern' enclosures the hedges tend to follow the lines of the original strips of land in the earlier farming system.

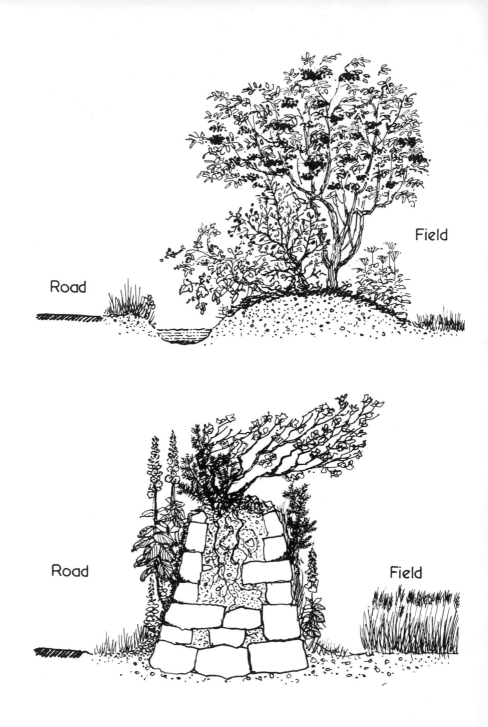

Road

Field

Road

Field

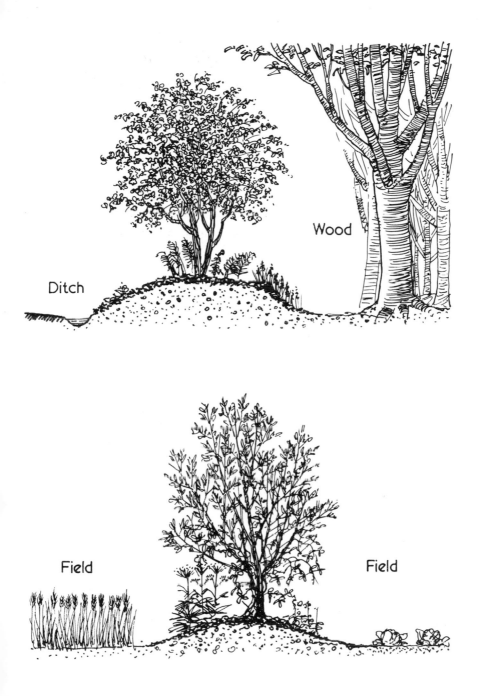

Ditch

Wood

Field

Field

Hedge Structure

Green hedgerows, for all their familiarity, are by no means a universal feature of the countryside of the British Isles; they are found mostly in England, and predominantly in lowland areas. In some other regions they are virtually absent. In hilly terrain in Wales, Derbyshire, Scotland and the Pennines they do exist, but are comparatively uncommon. Not only is it almost impossible for deep-rooted plants to become established in the shallow, often infertile soils in these areas, but constant battering by prevailing winds curtails their normal growth. As farmers cleared more land in upland areas, too, they had vast quantities of stones to dispose of: these they used for marking the boundaries of their estates, often as drystone walls.

Hedges in the west and north of the country, are best described as *sod banks*. Usually quite high and solidly built, the summit is topped

Boundary bank, with a few surviving trees (*Roy J. Westlake*)

with a row of shrubs, quite often gorse, which grows well on acid soil that will generally not support some of the species common on other soils. In areas of England where the soil is neutral or calcareous, we have what to the majority of people is the real definition of a hedge: an intermingled mixture of shrubs and herbs, dominated at irregular intervals by fine trees.

In Saxon times, when parish boundaries were being decided, a ditch was often dug by the local inhabitants. An earth bank was thrown up in the process, and, being raised and clearly marked it often formed the new roadway between one parish and the next. Today many of these *green streets* or *green lanes* are still used as bridleways; others have become overgrown with scrub, and hedges have become established on many of them.

When the farmer dug ditches to separate his land from that of his neighbours, the hedge was on the bank he threw up, and the ditch nearest to him. This was a legal necessity: the landowner could only take soil from his own land to build the bank. Thus it is the ditch and not the hedge which marks his boundary. Ditches were useful as drainage channels, and they often spread out into ponds, which provided water for the farmer's cattle. Today water for livestock is piped to fields, and so ditches are filled in, the water being drained by underground pipes.

The twisting lanes in many parts of Britain's countryside, originally bounded on either side by tall hedges, were generally the pathways linking one isolated farm with another, or one small hamlet with the next. These lanes were worn by feet from earlier times when men on horseback and on foot had to wend their way across the countryside to avoid trees, dense thickets, bogs and marshes.

3

Dating Hedges

Consistently old hedges are generally those which were recorded at the time of the Anglo-Saxon land charters. Often they were parish-boundary hedges, like the one found at Newnham, near Daventry in Northamptonshire. The age of this particular hedge was deduced by a local historian using Hooper's system (see below). By obtaining a copy of the appropriate Anglo-Saxon Charter, it was possible to follow part of the boundary hedge separating the parishes of Everdon and Newnham, and thus to check the results of the other system and date the hedge accurately.

Because of the difficulty in understanding many existing ancient charters, it is not always possible to follow the parish boundaries. The lack of clarity is understandable: it was generally only the local people who wanted to know where their boundaries were, and although, for example, references to the 'foul ditch' or the 'street' may not mean much to us a thousand years later, they were explicit enough at the time.

Hooper's System

Until recently there was no means of finding out how old a hedge was. Today this can be done with some accuracy, to within a hundred years or so. Dr Max Hooper, who has studied hedges for many years, was investigating the effects of pesticides and of the declining length of hedgerows on our bird life, when he accidentally came across his dating system.

The important fact in determining the age of a hedge is the number of shrubs found growing in it. Dr Hooper looked at a large number of hedges. His method is to count the number of different shrub species in a 33ft (30-metre) stretch of hedge. Where only one species is found, the hedge will be around 100 years old; if two species are growing there the hedge was 'planted' 200 years ago; if three species, 300, and so on. A hedge with ten species may have been in existence for a thousand years or more.

It must be remembered that this method does not apply to herbs, the smaller common plants of the hedge—brambles, nettles, and so on— but to those shrubs which, in their own right, will grow into trees or strong bushes: hawthorn, blackthorn, elder, holly, ash, horse-chestnut, etc.

Using Land Charters

It is very useful to have some means of verifying the age of the hedge. Both the earlier Anglo-Saxon land charters and the later Enclosure Acts and Awards have been used for this. The former have been collected together in Birch's *Cartularium Saxonium* and Kemble's *Codex Diplomaticus*, and the Enclosure Acts and Awards can be consulted at local Records offices.

Where a Saxon parish boundary hedge is known to exist, together with the original charter, the hedge age is 'known'. By counting the shrub species it is possible to see whether the number present tallies with the date given by the charter. A formula is used for determining the age once the species have been counted. Although a large number of hedges have been studied, the system is not perfect and a hedge thought to be 1,000 years old could vary by as much as two hundred years. Perhaps what the system really does is sort out hedges dating from different periods. A Saxon hedge can be pinpointed with reasonable accuracy, as can one planted as a result of the enclosures of the 1800s. But it is almost impossible to distinguish between hedges planted in the nineteenth and twentieth centuries.

Of course relatively few old charters exist, and those which have been discovered and used in hedge-dating are scattered over a wide area of the country. In Dr Hooper's survey only about 200 hedges were included, the ages of which were known, and these ranged from the south-west to the Midlands.

Local Variations

The differences in soils and climate, as well as the ways in which the hedges have been maintained, must to some extent affect the time needed for species to become established.

An interesting fact to emerge from these hedge studies was that some counties seem to have consistently older hedges than others. Many Devon hedges were found to be over 800 years old, whereas those in parts of Cambridgeshire and Lincolnshire were only one hundred years old. Yet in Kent, hedges with only a single species were rare, and most had at least three.

The richness of a hedge, the number of species present, was assumed to be due to the soil in which the plants of the hedge were growing. Chalk soils provided the right conditions for some plants to become well established, and fewer species managed to survive in areas where clays predominated. But information collected by D. Goose, and included in the *Flora of Wiltshire* (1957) did not seem to agree with such a theory. The book, compiled over many years, contained tables which indicated that in an old hedge on chalk soil there were twelve species of plants, and in a new one on similar soil only two. A similar count for a hedgerow on non-calcareous soil found ten species in an old hedge and two in a new one.

Dr Hooper's theory that one species would have become established in 100 years, two in 200 years and so on, was put to the test—with the help of Professor W. G. Hoskins—on hedges in Devon. One with two species was 140 years old; another with ten was 1,000 years old.

The theory has since been shown to work only on certain soils, and perhaps particularly on the hedges of lowland Britain. For it to work satisfactorily there must be enough shrubs growing. Sometimes this is not the case. Many fewer plants can tolerate acid soil conditions, or extreme climate, than neutral or chalky soil or moderate climate. So if shrubs are absent because they are unable to grow in the prevailing conditions, then the system is no longer workable.

No one has yet been able to state why, in reasonably good conditions, it has taken 100 years for one species to become established, 200 years for two species and so on. Nor is the particular species which becomes established after 100 years the same for every hedge. There is no predetermined order in which the plants will appear.

A lot more has to be understood about the way in which hedges grow up in the first place. Some interesting points have already arisen. It has been discovered that some trees will only be found in a hedge where a number of other species have already become established. For example, spindle (*Euonymus europaeus*) is usually only found in hedgerows which have six other shrub or tree species present: in other words, the hedge must be 600 years old before spindle will settle in. Field maple (*Acer campestre*) seems to occur in similar situations, though it will arrive earlier: there are usually four other species already established. Thus it seems that a hedge must be 400 years old before a maple will be found in it.

In some areas, local customs have dictated the composition of the hedgerows. For example, in parts of the Midlands damson trees have been planted in the hedges bordering some of the country lanes. These trees provide shelter for cattle and sheep during hot weather and also provide fruit. In other areas, including parts of Shropshire, the local tradition was to plant several species of trees and shrubs in the hedgerows: apple and holly, for instance, would be used along with the usual hawthorn or blackthorn. Sometimes when the farmer leased fields from the local landowner he was obliged to plant mixed hedges and the custom has survived in some counties where hedges have been planted in recent times. This practice obviously affects the accuracy of the dating system described earlier.

Clues From Boundaries

When trying to date hedges, any documentary evidence is invaluable. Although historians have speculated about boundaries put up during the Roman occupation, nothing is known for certain. It might eventually be possible to find the boundaries created by the Romans and, perhaps even more interesting and exciting, those put there by the Celts.

Boundaries were originally put up to separate counties, and these are some of the earliest for which we have any *documentary* evidence. Many counties first had boundaries in the ninth century. Landmarks already present, like streams, rivers and roads, are used, but often long artificial boundaries have had to be dug or made. Working in the field, local historians look for the remnants of these man-made stretches and then attempt to date what they find. The earliest boundaries for which there is some evidence, meagre as it may be, are in the south-west of England. The first boundary as far as we know that effectively separated Somerset from Devon (or vice versa!) dates from around the middle of the ninth century. Not surprisingly, boundaries around Somerset and Dorset, and Devon and Dorset, appeared at about the same time. A document for AD 870 informs us that Wiltshire first became a shire in that year. The very word 'shire' means 'to be cut off and marked out'. For many places, however, the information needed to date the boundary has been lost.

Anglo–Saxon Charters

By far the greatest surviving historical evidence of boundary markers is contained in the Anglo-Saxon land charters. As we have said, using some of the earlier charters it is very difficult to follow the boundary in the twentieth century. But later Saxon charters were much more specific, and gave a vast amount of information. Sometimes charters appear misleading, quoting earlier boundary dates; some may be forgeries, but it is likely that some boundaries were documented afresh at this time, even if an original one was created several hundreds of years earlier: as we do not have the earlier documentary evidence to confirm this it must remain a matter for conjecture.

Even where records of the boundaries do exist, the sceptics will ask how we can be sure that a hedge was planted at that time. Of course we cannot be absolutely sure, but it seems that having dug a ditch to mark a boundary, the landowners would have planted trees and shrubs on top of the bank to form a barrier, keeping out their neighbours' cattle and keeping in their own. It also seems likely that this kind of boundary, once it had grown, was much easier to see from a distance than a ditch or bank alone. Even if not planted, vegetation would often have grown up naturally on the bank, and in some areas would have given a fairly dense shrub-covering within a generation.

Date Your Own Hedge

You may want to go out and date your local hedges. There may not be a parish boundary hedge. However, do not choose just any hedge; try to find one which is irregular in line, because this often means that it is much older.

Having selected a hedge, and a suitable 33-ft (30-metre) stretch, count the species. You will then need the following simple formula for working out the age of this particular hedgerow:

Age of hedge in years − (99 × number of species)—16.

As you will see it is, as near as makes no difference, one species for each 100 years.

An Enclosure Act hedge is likely to consist mainly of one or two species, an older hedge will be well mixed, and a hedge with more than ten shrubs in a measured stretch probably goes back to the time of the Norman Conquest or earlier.

4

Farming and Hedges

It seems ironic that even before the final major Enclosure Act had been passed in 1903, people were questioning the need for hedges as a means of separating fields. Their main point was the large-scale wastage of valuable agricultural land. In the mid-1800s more than one-tenth of all land was found to be 'wasted' because of hedges, roadside verges and ditches.

It is difficult to give accurate figures for the length of demolished hedgerows but it is thought to be about 5,000 miles (over 8,000 km) every year. They have been disappearing slowly for many years now. In 1968 there were probably about 600,000 miles (960—970,000 km), and if we continue to uproot at the present rate, there will almost certainly be no hedgerows left in Britain by the beginning of the next century. However, because of the nature of farming in various parts of the country, it seems unlikely that this will happen. There will undoubtedly be vast tracts of hedgeless, prairie-like landscape, but they will be balanced by other areas with traditional hedgerows especially where sheep-farming is important.

Most hedges are 'farmers' hedges'. We may ourselves think of them as being important refuges for wildlife and aesthetically valuable assets in the countryside; but it is to the farmer that we must look—it is he who will decide on the fate of most of them. So the changes in our landscape pattern are due in the main to the continual evolution of the farming system. Although much work has been carried out, and we know that a vast range of wildlife species inhabit the hedges, we do not yet know the overall value, or even cost, of hedges to the farmer. Until recently no one really knew what effect the hedge had on the surrounding farmland, or how this affected the crop yield in the enclosed field. Nor is the effect of damage to hedges really known: stubble-burning is too often allowed to destroy sections of hedge, rain washes down earth banks exposing roots and removing animal or insect cover.

Changes in Britain's agricultural pattern have taken place gradually all through the centuries, although much more slowly in the past than today. It might seem reasonable to assume that the hedges in any particular field system all date from the same period, but this is not always true. Studies of field shapes and patterns have given rise to a number of ideas as to the origin of the shape of hedges in certain areas. Hedges of an elongated S shape are quite common in some parts of Britain, and probably result from the way in which the strips in earlier fields were ploughed. Most land had been 'hard-won' from woodland and scrub, and the farmer would want to cultivate as much of it as possible. If oxen went straight out at the end of a furrow, then a lot of ground was lost between the strips. However, if the oxen veered to the left as they neared the end of the strip, the space needed for the turnaround was far less. This system of strip-farming was

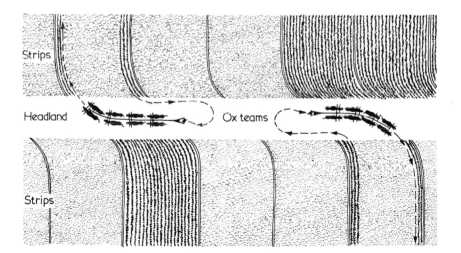

Strips

Headland   Ox teams

Strips

31

probably not practised after about 1400. From the time of the Tudors the idea was to plough straighter but somewhat narrower furrows. So it seems a reasonable assumption that the elongated S-shaped hedges date from before 1400. However, between the two World Wars, S-shaped strips of land were no longer grazed, because of the agricultural depression. Within a relatively short time hawthorn scrub grew up, which became managed as hedges when the land was again used, and so these features may be no more than about sixty years old.

Variations in Hedgerow Patterns

With greater changes taking place in farming in the seventeenth and eighteenth centuries, variations soon appeared in the hedgerow pattern. Initially the farming system was determined by the enclosures, the pieces of land allocated for various purposes, and as modern farming techniques developed some of these enclosed areas became unworkable or uneconomic. For example, the advent of Jethro Tull's seed drill meant that a greater area could be covered than by hand-sowing. Ploughing was improved and larger ploughs gave way to less cumbersome implements which speeded up the work. Furthermore, during the nineteenth century the rotation system of farming became characteristic of many parts of the country, so that smaller fields were established.

Yet at the same time modern machinery was being developed, which to be effective needed larger, not smaller, fields. It is always being said that hedge removal is a phenomenon of twentieth-century agricultural methods, but the idea was being pushed in the 1800s, though little uprooting was actually done: just how much is a matter for conjecture until older maps can be studied in detail. With cattle, sheep and a rotation system still dominant in many areas, hedges remained an accepted part of the farm.

The Industrial Revolution also contributed, less directly, to other changes in the farming pattern. Wool had been an important commodity, but because the new factory machines dealt efficiently with cheap imported cotton fibres, the demand for it started to decline. The large fields created in Tudor times for flocks of sheep were less suitable for arable farming at a time when horse-drawn equipment was still the general rule. An area of 20 acres (8 hectares) was much easier to manage than one of perhaps 100 acres (40 hectares).

Timber was needed in ever-increasing amounts as the Industrial Revolution got under way. Although oak has always been considered Britain's most important timber, elm was also grown extensively, being used for lock gates and water wheels, because it could withstand submersion in water without warping. Farmers planted many elm trees along their hedgerows, and as time went by their form often dominated the local country scene.

The Effects of the Farming Depression

In the farming depression of the early part of this century, many fields were left to go wild. Hedges in these areas were no longer managed and spread into the fields.

With the onset of World War II more home-grown food had to be produced, and surprisingly quickly every field was brought back into use. The attitude that as much land as possible is needed for agriculture has remained with us. Whereas in the past there was much common and waste land, today these areas have been enclosed as farming methods have increased in speed and efficiency. This has taken yet further the land enclosures of the eighteenth and nineteenth centuries instigated by Parliament to improve the efficiency of farming techniques. The old open-field system, characterised by its strip-farming, was highly inefficient, and extremely wasteful in both land and labour. These enclosures have given Britain her well-known twentieth-century landscape: one stipulation of the Enclosure Acts and Awards was that hedges had to be planted around the fields, to mark the new boundaries.

Changes in the Twentieth-century Landscape

Just as changes in agricultural methods led to enclosure in the eighteenth and nineteenth centuries, so the call for increased efficiency has led to the removal of enclosures in the twentieth century. Ever more machinery is used, and far fewer men are working the land. Large fields are needed for large machines, and in addition it has become difficult to spare the hand labour to manage hedgerows, a very time-consuming task. In many areas stock farming has declined or has changed to an intensive system, releasing land for growing arable crops. The investment required for sophisticated machinery, and ever-rising costs, have made farmers economy-conscious and anxious to plan their holdings as efficiently as possible. For most crops a field of about 50 acres (20 hectares) is a suitable unit.

In some areas, including parts of the Midlands, where cattle and sheep farming are of greater importance, smaller fields or 'paddocks' of between 5 and 10 acres (2 and 4 hectares) are preferred, although not universal. In such areas hedges may survive. Estimates made in the early 1970s showed, however, the kind of costs involved in hedge management:

Cutting and laying for stockproof hedge	£20 to £70 per 100m
Hand trimming	£2.90 to £19.90 per 100m
Mechanical trimming	30p to 90p per 100m

Removing each mile (1.6 km) of hedge costs about £200.

So not only is it extremely expensive to maintain hedges by the traditional method, but it also makes great demands on a diminishing band of farmworkers.

Effects on the landscape have been increased where the local hedges grew on banks and they too have been removed. In some cases the banks were originally built so that the hedge could be planted on top; in others the mound accumulated over the years, settling against the stems of the hedgerow trees and shrubs and gradually raising the height of the hedge. As mentioned earlier, in many fields it is the bank which distinctly and effectively marks the boundary. If the field pattern has to be changed then both hedge and ditch must be removed; where it is simply that the cost of maintaining the hedge is too high, then the hedge alone will be removed, often just chopped down, rather than grubbed out—not unlike the coppicing method. Where

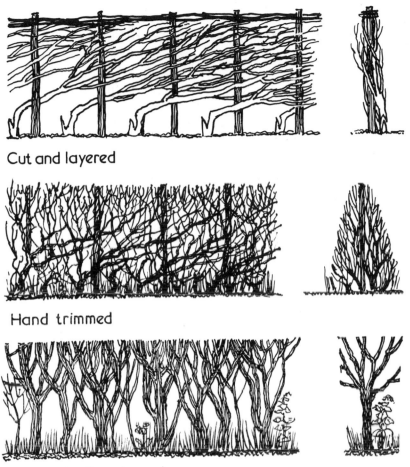

Cut and layered

Hand trimmed

Mechanically trimmed

the roots are not removed the hedge will grow up and the chopping-down procedure has to be repeated at regular intervals.

It has always been recognised that a great deal of valuable agricultural land has never been used, for a variety of reasons. Strip-farming caused great wastage, and probably more than one-fortieth of each field was never used because of headlands. In fields with an

Styles in stiles still seen in the countryside

irregular outline even more land is wasted at the headlands. Where hedges and hedgebanks are removed, not only is the 'lost' land recouped, but usually more as well.

Unmanaged hedges are not consistent with today's farming. They will spread into the surrounding fields, taking over more of the valuable land and also shading more of the crop, probably resulting in a lower yield in that part of the field.

Hedge Wildlife

Hedges are 'farmers' hedges' and what effect does the activity of the farming fraternity have on the wildlife living there? Thousands of years ago when Britain was covered with forest, all inland wildlife was adapted to live in wooded country; most of the birds were forest birds. As the woodland disappeared, at first very gradually, and then in recent times with ever-increasing rapidity, mammals, birds and insects with more or less success 'changed their ways' and moved to seek refuge in the hedgerows. It must be remembered that so many of these hedgerows, as features of the countryside, are relatively new.

Although conservationists and naturalists see the necessity for modern farming methods, nevertheless they still voice dismay, often vehemently, when discussing hedgerow removal. Their arguments usually tend to be emotional. Hedge removal in itself may not necessarily be a bad thing. Many hedges are so small and insignificant that their value as a wildlife refuge is dubious. Modern research has also shown that there are critical dimensions for hedges, and some may even have an adverse effect on wildlife. Although a decreasing amount of territory could lead to a reduction in the bird population, a smaller length of *correctly maintained* hedge will often be of more value to wildlife than a long strip of thin unsuitable hedge.

There is an average of fifteen birds' nests to a mile of hedge. If, as has been suggested, 5,000 miles (8,000 km) have been disappearing annually, no fewer than 150,000 (75,000 pairs) of birds must have been displaced. What happened to the birds? Did they in fact 'vanish'? The answer seems to be that they have had the resilience to build their nests closer together, with up to 80 per mile being recorded.

Where it has been difficult to enlarge fields, possibly because of the nature of the terrain, as in the aerial photograph, the smaller units with their accompanying hedges remain an important refuge for wildlife. Even with the advent of modern machinery, there are still areas where it is not possible to divide the land into fields and grow crops (*Aerofilms*)

The density for birds must reach a maximum, however: there must come a point at which they will crowd together no tighter. Though the birds managed with less hedge in some areas, in other places their numbers did decrease. Various factors will have influenced this, not least being the make-up of the particular hedge. Most birds need hedges which provide a dense cover to protect the nest, and later the

39

young, against would-be predators. Hawthorn and blackthorn hedging provides much more efficient cover than many species in mixed hedges.

Soil Erosion Defences

One argument with which conservationists often defend hedgerows is that they prevent windblows, such as those experienced in the Fens. Fenland regions have never been particularly well endowed with hedgerows, and since they are subject to the most frequent blowouts the argument is unconvincing. Fields in the Fens have usually been divided by drains, necessary in earlier times to collect and carry away surface water. Hedges were often difficult to grow because of the marshy nature of the original land. Where prudent farmers have planted hedges, it does seem likely that these have helped to reduce the effects of windblows.

The problem of soil erosion has increased, but this is due to new farming methods, not to hedge-grubbing. The farmer has to prepare a fine seedbed early in the year. As soon as possible after this the land is sprayed to get rid of weeds. So in a dry spring, it is certain that soil blows will be a continuous threat, particularly in hedgeless areas, including a great part of the intensively farmed area of lowland Britain. Some hedges will prevent soil blows; others will not. The effectiveness of hedges as windbreaks is, as would be expected, dependent on a number of factors, such as their height, thickness and density.

Facing page (*above*) The Fenland region of eastern England, much of which has only been reclaimed from marsh in the last 100 years or so, was never hedge country; the fields were separated by drainage ditches, which until the advent of piped drainage systems carried the water from the fields. The larger, more regularly shaped fields are easier to farm than smaller, irregular units (*Aerofilms*)

(*below*) There are areas in the Fenland region, as exhibited here, where woodlands and hedgerows feature in the landscape. The regular-shaped fields are again shown, and some of this system probably dates from the drainage period, when these units were easier to manage. In contrast, the landscape does not appear so 'barren' (*Aerofilms*)

Hedge damaged by stubble-burning (*Goodman Photographics*)

Rain and frost can also be enemies, eroding hedgebanks, especially in narrow lanes where large vehicles have already cut them back (*Goodman Photographics*)

Sometimes a hedge can effectively stop the wind up to a distance of forty times its own height, on the leeward side, as well as a maximum of twice its own height on the windward side. Furthermore in areas like East Anglia, where soil erosion is a particular hazard, a hedge may reduce the erosion by up to fifteen times its height on the leeward side. In other words, if a hedge is 10ft (3m) high, then erosion will either not occur, or be drastically reduced, up to 150ft (50m) from the hedge.

High hawthorn hedges have been encouraged in some areas where hops are grown, because they form an effective windbreak. This is necessary because the hops will have grown tall by the beginning of September.

For sheep farmers hedges act as protection against the wind during the lambing season. In addition, in open areas where the wind can blow across large tracts of countryside, hedges trap snow and so protect roads and lanes from being blocked; in places where hedges have been uprooted, it is often necessary to put up lengths of snow fence instead.

Damage to Hedges

Hedges are often unintentionally damaged by various farming activities. Straw- and stubble-burning, although subject to a voluntary straw-burning code, is often practised when conditions are unsuitable: in too strong a wind or with the wind from the wrong direction. Hedges can be so badly damaged that they are unable to regenerate, and then they are later uprooted; some are replaced by fences; others are not, because they were not apparently useful.

There can be considerable and widespread drifting when herbicides are sprayed on to field crops, and this is particularly true when spraying is done from the air. Even on a relatively still day, the drift from crop-spraying, especially from helicopters and aeroplanes, can be far-reaching, causing untold damage to the hedge and its plant life.

5

The Hedgerow Nature Reserve

A barren wasteland devoid of trees and hedges, with vast expanses of almost sterile countryside, stretching as far as the eye can see, punctuated by those lofty, metal monstrosities known as pylons; a wildlife desert in an arable paradise. This is an apt description of a large area of eastern England.

Although much work has yet to be carried out, the hedgerow as a nature reserve must be of great importance to many forms of wildlife living in our islands. As we have seen, it has been estimated that hedgerows extend for about 600,000 miles (say 965,000 km); the average width is about 6ft, which gives a total area of 436,000 acres (176,442 hectares): a greater area than all the nature reserves put together. The amount of hedgerow varies from region to region. Whereas Devon has 25 miles (40 km) of hedge to every square kilometre of land, in Cambridgeshire there is only 10 miles (16 km) in the same area.

Like any other habitat, each hedge is unique, with its own collection of plant and animal life. Nevertheless, we can gain some indication of the importance of hedgerows to plants and animals by looking at some of the species which are to be found in their intricately interwoven expanse.

Within the tangle of plants at the bottom of the hedge, voles and shrews may have their runs, crossing and criss-crossing in a complex

Steep hedgebanks, still found in many parts of the country away from main roads, encourage a wide range of plants to grow. Such areas provide food as well as shelter for a variety of wildlife, from the smallest invertebrates to the larger mammals (*D. F. Wright*)

labyrinth of underground tunnels. The rabbit finds a home here, excavating the hedge bank to make his tunnel, safe from predators lurking above the hedge's green ribbon of life—though only sometimes safe from stoat or weasel breeding in the hedge bottom. Lizards can be seen basking on a warm sunlit day, easy prey to a marauding bird looking for a much-needed meal. On the leaves, caterpillars hungrily devour the greenery, taking their share of nourishment, vital links in the sophisticated and complicated hedgerow food chain. Snails saunter slowly along, as if they have all the time in the world to eat their food and lay their eggs, unaware of the sharp beak of a thrush waiting to smash open their shells and energetically extricate their soft bodies. These smaller animals, snails, slugs and caterpillars and an unending list of other invertebrates, indeed provide valuable food for birds and their hungry chicks, waiting in a warm nest in the hedgerow bushes, their mouths agape for nourishment.

During the day a wide range of wildlife will have been active, and as the daylight fades, and the shadows of dusk creep over the now silent fields, nocturnal species will make their entrance, both prey and predators. Foxes will come on their nightly patrols in search of food. Owls swoop silently from a darkened sky to seize an unsuspecting shrew in ever-eager talons. Moths flit by and stop to suck the sweet-tasting nectar from hedgerow plants, or to lay their eggs on a suitable stem or leaf. More than likely many of them will not see the following night, grabbed on the wing by a fluttering bat, its diet consisting solely of night-flying insects. Down in the hedgerow bottom, protected by the long herbs, the hedgehog snuffles and grunts as it constantly searches for grubs, abundant amongst the rich, green vegetation.

Here is a whole world of wildlife of which few people are aware. Together with its links with the surrounding countryside, the hedge plays a very important part in the balance of nature.

The make-up of hedgerows and the plants they contain are important factors in determining not only which bird species but to a certain extent which other animals are found there. Where hawthorn predominates, the main birds to benefit will be seed-eating species which appreciate the crop of haws in autumn—especially the thrushes, like the migrant fieldfares and redwings. The innumerable species of herbs

A luxuriant wildlife habitat: overgrown ditch and mixed vegetation, with a wide verge (*Goodman Photographics*)

in the hedge, as opposed to trees and shrubs, offer other seeds; the oak provides acorns for squirrels.

Any hedgerow, especially one with a mixed and varied flora, supports a wealth of invertebrate life—an important part of the closely knit and interdependent hedge ecosystem. Many insects like a dampish habitat, and the hedge bottom, often with accompanying ditch, is ideal. For those that prefer the sunny edges of woodlands, the hedgerow provides the same conditions, and includes many of the same shrubs—it may even be a remnant of otherwise cleared woodland. The food plants for many butterflies and moths, for instance, are readily available; and as the caterpillars hatch, some of them in turn provide food for insectivorous birds.

Few of all these thousands of creatures are seen by any but particularly discerning and informed observers. The most noticeable are of course the larger day-flying insects, butterflies, wasps and bees, and the hover-flies so often mistaken for bees. At night, the moths which crash into

47

the headlights of passing cars attract our attention, but in the daytime most of these sit inactive and quiet within the security of the densely interwoven hedge foliage.

Through the seasons' cycle, the threads of life that make up the hedgerow system are kept going one way or another. During autumn and winter most mixed hedges are more or less leafless, except for the occasional holly bush, and the insect population is much reduced. However, vast numbers of over-wintering species are to be found in among the thickly interwoven twigs and branches, even if many fall prey to hungry birds.

Spring is the particularly active period. The majority of hedgerow shrubs burst into leaf earlier in the year than the dominating trees, one of the first to become conspicuous being the hazel, its pendulous pollen-laden catkins attracting early insect visitors. Blackthorn also flowers early. The greatest period of growth seems to be that preceding the flowering period, and because the plant is probably at its most nutritious, rich with sap, just then, the invertebrates find plenty of food. Once the flowers have faded, the peak in the annual life of the shrub is reached. Nutrients were obtained in vast quantities from the soil earlier, to manufacture food for growth, but less is needed once the flowers have been formed and, with luck, pollinated by those hordes of insects. It is the hedgerow flowers that attract the invertebrates to the hedge at this time of the year, to their own benefit.

Of the hedge plants particularly valuable as food for insects, the most common hedging shrub, the hawthorn, is again the most obvious. Entomologists have estimated that at least one hundred different species of moth caterpillars feed on hawthorn shoots and leaves in spring. One of the other common hedge species frequently eaten by caterpillars is blackthorn; about two hundred species use this shrub as a source of food. Moths make use of a wide range of the possible habitats within the hedge. The caterpillars of some species will actually burrow into the fleshy parts of the leaves; others will stay, well camouflaged but detectable, on the leaves themselves. Some moths overwinter in the larval stage—as caterpillars, rather than as eggs laid on leaves or shoots, or as pupae fastened to stems or buried among the dead leaves and soil at the hedge bottom. Overwintering caterpillars have to withstand the rigours of hard weather, but if they succeed they will have an advantage in the spring, being ready to feed and resume growth as soon as conditions are right. Most species are kept in close check by climate and predators, and it is only occasionally that a species attracts attention by reaching plague proportions.

Chief of the pollinators for the spring and summer flowers in hedgerows and accompanying roadside verges are the bees, which use the nectar to make honey to feed their offspring. Umbelliferous plants like cow parsley or hogweed, with their large masses of flower heads, provide a suitable food source for many species. The flowers of the earliest shrubs fade and others, particularly climbing herbs like honeysuckle and bryony, take over as the food supply for the visiting, as well as the resident, invertebrates.

The spring hedgerow is full of intense activity. The first flowers push their heads above the soil which only a few weeks earlier was totally hostile. The green leaves of the early flowering celandine are closely followed by the burnished gold of its buttercup-like flowers. Bees out early in search of food will hover gently, the slight buzz from their wings giving away their presence. As the sun increases its power, the once-cold soil is gradually warmed and inert plants and animals begin to stir. Plants vie with each other for the best position, the weaker species often pushed out by competitors. Mid- to late May brings the hawthorn flowers, and summer comes, bringing the hedgerow into full life. Foliage now thick, lush and green acts as cover for the myriads of little residents and visitors, including grasshoppers and those ever-munching caterpillars of moths and butterflies. Grasses, whose delicate heads are at times almost stationary in stagnant summer air, at other times bend and dance in strong summer winds, or sway gently in softer breezes. Some grasses grow close to the hedge bottom; others reach up and become interwoven amongst taller hedgerow plants.

A female red admiral butterfly alights on a nettle plant, depositing her eggs on the upper surface of the leaves. Here they will hatch and those that escape the sharp eyes of hedge-hunting birds may reach pupation stage within a few weeks.

A family of young weasels has been born, but as yet has not seen the outside world. The mother tends them carefully, protecting them under the hedgerow's shelter, but in a few weeks they will probably be dead, her care 'wasted' as some bird of prey swoops down and takes them in its sharp talons. She herself feeds on the mice and voles, rabbits and birds' eggs, around her.

In the bottom of the hedge the partridge has been incubating her eggs, the young eventually breaking their way out of the claustrophobic though protective shell. The creamy-white clusters of hawthorn flowers, once pollinated, start to change to the well-known haws. Wild roses seek support in the hedge, their large flowers attracting many insects. From April to July there will be a successive and almost continuous white bloom from the umbellifers, including the first to flower, cow parsley, followed by rough chervil, and later by hedge parsley.

Bird life too has its hectic cycle and where there are mixed hedges there are many birds. The yellowhammer dashes from a hedge at one side of a country lane to shelter on the other side. In the taller trees are the nests of a number of species, including larger ones such as rooks, jackdaws and magpies. Chaffinches seek out hedgerow trees for use as song posts and tree sparrows will make their nests in holes in the trunks.

Hidden in the twisted tangle of undergrowth at the hedge bottom, a little-known underworld, smaller animals like voles and shrews seek out relative safety. Where there is plenty of food in nearby fields, rabbits will live and breed in the sanctuary of the hedge. The hedgehog lies hidden in the hedgerow during the day, and comes out snorting and snuffling on its way at night.

All too soon it is autumn and with the shorter, colder days, gradual changes take place in the hedgerow. Animals have bred and plants produced their seeds in the press for survival. Now leaves start to wither and growth for most species has stopped. But autumn is the time to see one group of plants which have remained relatively inactive during the preceding months: fungi, most with dome-shaped caps, like the shaggy ink-cap, will rapidly grow and fruit, producing a multitude of spores.

Dew-encrusted cobwebs sparkle and glint on mornings of autumn sunlight, shining lines seemingly stretched between all possible hedge-row twigs: perhaps at this time of year, with the hedgerow much

The barn owl, not always sleepy, will swoop down on small hedgerow animals with silent precision (*S. James*)

quieter, it is easier for the spiders to keep webs intact. Hoar frost on sharp mornings settles silently on every blade and shoot, giving the hedgerow a blurred and beautiful outline.

Winter, and the hedgerow is in a restful state. To many it may seem dead and lifeless, most of the trees and shrubs naked, many of the low-growing plants absent or alive only underground. But on days when a crisp covering of snow lies over the ground, it is obvious that the hedge is still a centre of life. The tracks of hungry birds lead in and out, where nuts and fruits, shed from the trees, have fallen, or where berries still cling to the branches of hawthorn and rose.

Stoat and weasel, mole, vole and mouse, still have their indeterminable maze of runs and tunnels in the hedgerow jungle. Not that all hedges are hospitable habitats: those high on a hill, sparse of cover, battered and lashed by gale-force winds which rip between the stems of the few plants established there provide but poor shelter.

At no time of year is the hedgerow an isolated ecological unit. Animals and birds come in from surrounding areas to feed, seeds blow in from other places and may take root, insects, like the colourful butterflies that lay their eggs on hedgerow plants, will flutter off elsewhere to feed and all too soon to die. A badger prowls in from a nearby sett and rips open the wasps' nest, so carefully constructed in spring, and in summer a seething mass of life, to eat the wriggling grubs. Bumble bees come in to take over the deserted nests of mice or wrens.

The migrating birds which nest here take off in autumn for winter quarters perhaps thousands of miles away. Some of the hardier species will remain all year, but those which found cover in spring will find the winter hedge exposed and inhospitable, as autumn passes into winter. There was plenty of food in the breeding season, with plants flourishing, birds, mammals and insects rearing their young, the food chain unbroken: now many links are dead or have gone, and there is less chance of a meal.

Three main, though not always distinct, groups of animals use the hedgerow. Some species are resident, living and breeding here—as do the plants. Many different birds are resident, as well as the mice and voles, rabbits and hedgehogs, insect larvae, snails and lizards. Other species are regular visitors although they live and breed elsewhere: butterflies and moths, owls and other birds of prey, weasels, stoats and foxes will be recorded. Sometimes a regular visitor may take up residence: an owl, for instance, finds a suitable hole in a tree, so nests and rears its young there. Then there are occasional, even accidental, visitors—birds, mammals, snakes: they come in search of food when their own supply has failed or their habitat has been disturbed or destroyed.

6

Hedgerow Trees and Shrubs

Hedgerows have been a feature of our landscape in one form or another for a thousand years, and whether by sown seeds, or by man's careful strategy, trees have always featured in their make-up. The older Saxon boundary hedges will probably support the oldest timber; the Enclosure hedges the youngest. But what do we know of these majestic hedgerow trees? In 1951 it was found that England had around 56,000,000 hedgerow and park trees, about one to every acre. The more established timber was found in the south of the country, and larger saplings in the north.

As far as stocks of trees were concerned the survey caused a stir. It was generally recognised that for every large tree counted, there should be two medium-sized specimens, three small ones and six saplings. But the situation was far removed from this ideal. Although various recommendations were made, most were ignored. Not surprisingly when a similar survey was undertaken in 1965 things had gone from bad to worse, with the loss of millions of trees in the intervening fourteen years.

To encourage people to become concerned about trees, too often taken for granted as a natural and permanent part of the landscape, Plant A Tree Year was launched in 1973. The Tree Council was formed as a result, to encourage people to plant trees and to organise surveys to enable the distribution of major species to be mapped. To coincide

Dead, smothered with ivy—still a useful food source, but no one now is likely to replace this old hedgerow oak in an over-tidy hedge (*R. Armstrong*)

with the first National Tree Week held in 1975—now an annual event —the Council started an important tree survey which is expected to take several years to complete. Given time, country lovers will be able to help by listing every tree to be found in hedgerows, shelter-belts and small woodlands in their locality. Details can be obtained from the

Tree Council. We already know enough about the distribution of trees in large woods and forests. But the Tree Council survey, besides pinpointing the site of each tree, will also aim to discover the state of the particular species and its health. It will eventually show areas where trees are particularly needed, and hedgerows are likely to be highlighted as valuable sites for establishing new trees, adding visual and aesthetic impact to the countryside, breaking up areas that have become stark and barren.

Tree Species in Hedges

Most of the trees which occur naturally in hedgerows are deciduous species, shedding their leaves in autumn. Evergreen species do occur, including the holly which, although only of shrub-like stature in many hedges, grows to tree height in some places. Because Britain was at one time almost completely covered with woodland, many of the trees found are woodland species. Very rarely is a hedgerow tree older than the hedge where it grows.

Some hedgerow trees have been planted by wise, canny and erudite landowners, and others have simply seeded themselves and become established; some species will only be found when the hedge has reached a certain age. One can only assume that the environmental conditions necessary for these trees to flourish within the hedge only come about at this stage. Oak (*Quercus spp*), so important to our ancestors, particularly for ship-building, although 'England's Tree' is much less common than previously. The elms (*Ulmus spp*) have suffered devastation as a result of epidemic outbreaks of Dutch Elm Disease, although they may be re-establishing themselves in some areas by means of suckers arising from the felled tree.

Despite recent interest in hedges we still need to know a great deal more about distribution of species, their longevity and so on. So surveys like that carried out in Cambridgeshire by the local Naturalists' Trust are often very enlightening. For that survey the hedges in the county were divided into three main categories—pure hedges, 'mild' mixed hedges and mixed hedges.

PURE HEDGES

Because of the make-up of the pure hedges in Cambridgeshire, it was thought necessary to subdivide them into two groups, according to their dominant species. As with many other areas, thorn hedges were the commonest. The two major species in the pure thorn hedges were, predictably, hawthorn (*Crataegus monogyna*) and blackthorn (*Prunus spinosa*). In some of the hedges classified as pure, other species were present, including elder (*Sambucus nigra*), rose (*Rosa spp*) and ash (*Fraxinus excelsior*). The survey, which used Hooper's dating system so that comparisons could be made with other areas, found that most of the hedges had been planted during the last two hundred years.

In the second group of pure hedges, elm (*Ulmus spp*) was the main species. Smooth-leaved elm (*Ulmus carpinifolia*), known in some places as suckering elm, was the dominant tree. This elm is generally confined to the eastern counties of England, and in Cambridgeshire these elm hedges were considered to be abundant. Smooth-leaved elm produces a large number of suckers which spread quite rapidly in many directions to form a hedge. Elm hedges often owe their existence to one elm having produced a remarkable length of sucker growth. Most of the hedges in Cambridgeshire occurred around the old enclosures, and had been established on the heavy soils.

One of the noticeable features was that few other species were associated with this particular tree, although one or two other trees, including spindle (*Euonymus europaeus*) and hornbeam (*Carpinus betulus*), were also noted.

'MILD' MIXED HEDGES

It was suggested that these hedges, containing two or three tree or shrub species per 30-metre stretch, were deliberately planted, just before during or just after the Tudor period. Over a span of more than four hundred years from the 1500s, 'mild' mixed hedges have generally developed an interesting mixture of plants. Although there were some

(*Overleaf*) A well-kept stockproof hedge—but more trees would enliven a bleak scene and add to its potential for wildlife (*Mick Hales*)

noticeable variations, one of the most characteristic trees in such hedges was the field maple (*Acer campestre*).

Hedges which have a number of different shrubs spread all along them fall into this category. Among the species noted were dogwood (*Cornus sanguinea*), hazel (*Corylus avellana*) and guelder rose (*Viburnum opulus*). An interesting fact to emerge from the survey was that these species are generally associated with very old woodlands. The hedges in which they are found are therefore, in general terms, very old relics of the countryside. Many are woodland assarts, and these often contain herbs typical of woodland flora, including dog's mercury (*Mercuralis perennis*), which was found in many instances. Where records exist for old mixed hedges, most have been found to be parish boundaries and are very ancient.

The survey showed, not unexpectedly, that thorn hedges were usually planted and mixed hedges were usually 'natural'—the latter containing a number of typical woodland species. Many of the Cambridgeshire natural hedges were poor in variety of species. Mixed hedges had a poor distribution of tall herbs: as few as four species were recorded. Yet in a rich thorn hedge there were as many as eight. This contradicts the often-held belief that mixed hedges have a more varied flora than thorn ones.

Some interesting, if somewhat tentative, conclusions emerge from the Cambridgeshire survey. For example, pure hedges were considered not worthy of preservation, on two counts: first, they were relatively recent, and so did not provide a suitable habitat for very many species; and second, they were too common to be in danger of disappearing completely. Both hawthorn and blackthorn hedges fell into this category.

From the point of view of wildlife conservation, mixed hedges were found to be the most important. They are older (usually, although not universally), have a richer flora and fauna, and are relatively rare in the county.

Other naturalists' trusts are also collecting records of their hedgerow flora and fauna, and further information is available from farm surveys undertaken by the Farming and Wildlife Advisory Service. Under this scheme two surveys carried out on two Lincolnshire farms have pinpointed the main species. Here the commonest hedge shrub was generally hawthorn. In some cases elder made up a good proportion; in others it was elm. In two instances a greater number of herb species were found in clipped hedges than in unclipped ones: 34 unclipped to 46 clipped in one example, and in the other example 23 to 38 respectively.

Hedgerow Trees

ASH (*Fraxinus excelsior*)
Although the ash is widespread, growing on a variety of soils, it does particularly well on limestone, especially in sheltered, lowland areas. Ash was extensively planted in the pre-Enclosure hedges, the good supply of timber being used for tools, fencing posts and hurdles as well as for fuel.

A young ash tree has smooth grey bark, but as the tree grows and matures it has a ribbed surface, reminiscent of a fish-net. The distinctive jet-black buds of the ash, very hard and with a dull sooty appearance when compared with the shiny surface of some other species, are arranged in opposite pairs on the stout twigs and are instantly identifiable. In winter the thickness of the twigs is conspicuous: the size of the compound leaves once they appear demands strong support in high winds and heavy rain. The lance-shaped, tooth-edged leaflets are each as large as the leaves of some other trees, ranging up to about 3in (7.5cm) long. They appear later than those of most other species, at the end of April or the beginning of May.

The ash forms large numbers of winged seeds, commonly known as 'keys' from their resemblance to the keys used in medieval locks. On its single twisted wing, a seed will be blown some distance to lie dormant on, or just in, the soil until the following spring. Competition for space, and the ravages of grazing animals, dictate that few will grow to more than a few inches, and the majority of those that fell close to the parent tree are doomed. A few that land, by various means, further afield may reach mature status many years hence.

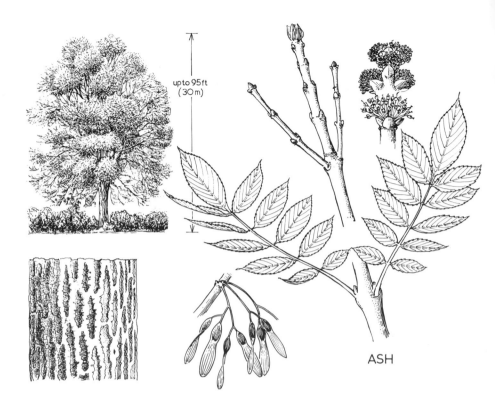

ASH

The name 'ash' comes from the Anglo-Saxon *aesc* and the Scandinavian *ask*. Records of the ancient laws of Howell Dda from Wales show that it was known then as *onnen*.

Along with the oak and elm, the ash is among the most useful of Britain's many species of trees. Although its wood has now been replaced in the main by metal, in the past it was used in a wide variety of ways, especially for tool handles. A Roman iron implement, dating from the first century AD, unearthed from a Roman settlement at Caerleon in Gwent, was found to have a handle made of ash. It is still used for hockey sticks, oars, paddles, rudders, billiard cues, cricket stumps and polo sticks, amongst other things, having a springy resilience that modern plastics cannot equal. The wood is also used for policemen's truncheons!

One reason why it is now less often grown as an ornamental tree is that it has a 'noxious drip' and casts a deep shade; few species of plants can compete with its overwhelming size and its mass of fibrous roots, which stretch over a considerable area beneath the surface and take the moisture from the soil.

Because of its earlier value and widespread distribution in the countryside the ash features widely in folklore and early legend. It has been considered one of the most magical and valuable of Britain's trees, and has many connections with the affairs of love; in Yorkshire for example, with a leaf from an ash tree tucked under her pillow, a girl would recite the following:

> Even-ash, even-ash I pluck thee,
> This night my true love to see.
> Neither in his rick nor in his rare,
> But in the clothes he everyday wear.

According to tradition, once the rhyme had been repeated, the girl's future husband would appear to her, as if by magic.

Ash burns green or dry; John Evelyn called it the sweetest of our forest fuelling and the fittest for ladies' chambers, because of the fragrance it gives off when burning.

It was perhaps the ash which was the *yggdrasil* or world-tree, featured in the mythology of Scandinavia. Pliny suggested that its leaves were so effective at keeping serpents at bay that they would even keep clear of the shadows it cast. In Devon, if the wood of the ash was burned at Christmastide, it was supposed to keep the devil at a distance. Also, according to tradition, it was by a fire made from the twigs of ash that Mary first bathed the young Christ child. In his *Flora Scotica* (1777), the Scottish author John Lightfoot noted an odd custom: as soon as a new-born child arrived the midwife or nurse would push a green ash-twig into the fire in the room. The sap exuding from the end was collected in a spoon and given to the baby—his first liquid after birth. Ash was considered a 'strong' tree, and this was seen as transferring some of the strength of the tree to the new arrival. In other areas it was thought to protect him against witchcraft.

63

BEECH (*Fagus sylvatica*)

A fully grown beech, its trunk clothed in smooth silver-grey bark, will tower above the other hedgerow species, and at its greatest will reach a height of over 100ft—about 30m. At this maximum growth its trunk will have a girth of nearly 20ft (6m). Where the tree grows in the open, in a hedgerow or park as opposed to a wood, it has a rounded crown with slender pendulous branches.

The slim bright-brown buds are arranged alternately along the twigs. In spring they are long, glossy and pointed; then in late April, the leaf, neatly folded fanwise beneath the protective scales, extricates itself and takes on an oval shape. Pale green at first, the leaves gradually become shinier and a deeper colour, their wavy margins enhanced by a fine fringe of gossamer-like down. In the early days of summer they have an almost transparent appearance.

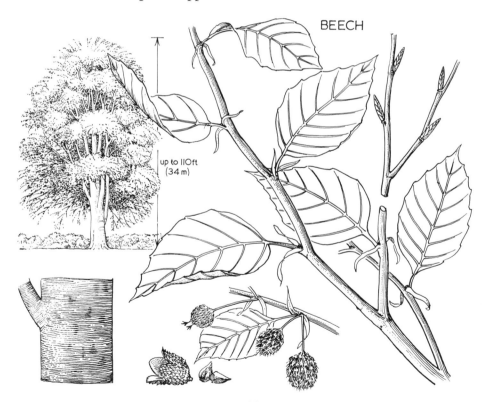

BEECH

up to 110ft
(34 m)

64

Autumn comes and the leaves change first to orange and then to a reddish-brown. As the gentle rays at sunset catch the vivid colours of the autumn beech they give it a glowing aurora, unsurpassed by anything else in nature.

At about the same time as the leaves open, the flowers appear, male and female blossoms on each tree. Groups of male catkins grow together, each consisting of a purplish-brown round tassel, made up of about fifteen green-coloured flowers bearing conspicuous yellow anthers. Pollination is generally brought about by the wind. Female flowers usually appear in pairs, surrounded by a cupule made up of several overlapping scales. Later these scales will form the four-lobed husk which protects the nut, and this will eventually split. The 'nut' inside is known as mast. In some years a large crop of this is produced, to the benefit of many birds and animals. Some years see almost no nuts at all. There is no known pattern to this, although a five-to-eight-yearly cycle of abundant crops seems most usual; this period may be extended, with large yields only occurring at nine-to-twelve-year intervals. The tree may have to grow for fifty or more years in the hedgerow before cropping.

Country folk have found the fallen beech mast a valuable food for their swine, which would be let loose in beechwoods in autumn. But the erratic cropping must have left the swine sadly thin in some years! Now that methods of livestock husbandry are less casual, it is the wild animals and birds of the hedgerow and forest the tits, squirrels, mice, deer and badgers—that eagerly seek out the nut, rich in nutritious oil. The tree also feeds the larvae of many insects—witness the punctured leaves in summer.

Although the beech occurs as a native species on chalk and limestone in the south-eastern part of the country, it has been planted in so many other areas, from early times, that it is widely distributed. Modern research in peat deposits has shown that Julius Caesar's statement that no beech trees grew in Britain was mistaken. Beckwith in Yorkshire takes its name from Becwudo, 'beech wood', reflecting the fact that the tree was planted there as far back as AD 792.

Although the timber is stronger than oak it is less durable, and so it has not been used so extensively. It does survive well under water, and

An attractive beech hedge in a garden—green in summer, warm brown in winter. An effective windbreak but a slow grower (*Mick Hales*)

has been used for bridge piles: beech and alder piles can be found beneath the old Waterloo Bridge in London. Millers found the wood suitable for their sluices. Built shortly after the Norman Conquest, Winchester Cathedral's massive structure is supported on piles made from beech timber. Heavy, hard and fairly easily worked, it has also been used for furniture. Pale brown in colour, the surface is broken by a series of lines and irregular blotches showing up as darker tints.

Beech hedging occurs in the South-west, the leaves clinging on with warm beauty long after they turn brown. But the most famous beech hedge is at Meikleour, in Perthshire, Scotland. It stretches for a quarter of a mile (400m) and is about 90ft (27m) high with no less than six hundred trees in it.

CRAB APPLE (*Malus sylvestris*)
To an extraordinary extent people have ignored the wild fruits of the

countryside—until recently. With the swing towards organically-grown and whole foods, food-for-free is in again. The crab apple has regained its own. As a wild hedgerow tree, it is still quite common in many parts of the countryside. In areas with other apple trees, it may be difficult to decide whether the tree is truly wild or whether it has strayed from a nearby orchard.

The small purple buds, covered with grey hairs, burst open in April to reveal the bright green leaves, 1–2in (2.5–5cm) long. Both upper and lower surfaces are usually smooth, although occasionally the latter may be covered with fine hairs.

The small umbel-like flowers, sweet-scented, pink-streaked and borne in clusters, appear in May, the tree at this time being one of the most beautiful in the countryside. Its crooked branches and long irregular shoots add much to its character. Richard Jefferies remarked that 'the old hedge-crab—the common despised crab-apple—in spring is covered with blossom, such a mass of blossom that it may be distinguished a mile away' (*Trees in Towns*). By autumn in a good year the flowers, long since faded, will have given rise to crimson fruits, just over an inch (3cm or so) across and of mouth-puckering sourness. It has now been remembered that crab jelly used to be a country delicacy (some would say an acquired taste). If the fruit is mixed with blackberries or even the berries of rowan (mountain ash), a delicious jelly certainly results.

To make ordinary crab-apple jelly, the fruits are gathered in autumn, and stewed. The resulting pulp is passed through a fine sieve (or strained through a jelly bag), sugar is added, and the whole boiled. Sometimes the rotting crab apples are still collected and used for cider-making. A vinegar, known as vargis or verjuice, was once made in the country from crabs. A few crab apples were also added to tarts to improve the flavour, and crab-apple wine is quite potent.

Children are often tempted to taste the apples, although the abundance of malic acid will effectively stop them from eating much! Pigs relish crabs, and their ancestor, the wild boar, fed on them in the wild.

The crab-apple of the hedgerow will grow almost anywhere with good soil. When fully grown the tree may reach anything up to 50ft (16m) or so, although old trees which are still no more than tall bushes are not unusual, such is the variety of growth and form. The tree can be distinguished from its cultivated relative mainly by its rounded crown: orchard apple trees tend to be pyramidal in shape. Also, again unlike the commercially grown apple tree, the crab's crown spreads extensively; in some examples the spread is greater than the height! Although the brown bark has an almost smooth texture in young trees, as they age it takes on a more cracked and fissured appearance.

The crab-apple is probably native to Britain, extending as far north as the Clyde coast of Scotland. It is widely distributed over much of Europe, and has been known for almost as long as man has been around. Most of the apple trees now cultivated in Britain owe their existence to, and have evolved from, the crab-apple. Even today the stock is still used for grafting purposes.

The wood of the tree has a very hard, close, fine-grained texture, and so in earlier times it was suitable for mallets and screws. Before the days of imported timber the wood of the crab, as well as of the cultivated apple, was much prized by wood-carvers.

The name 'crab' comes from a word used in the lowland areas of Scotland, *scrab*, in its turn a corruption of a much earlier Anglo-Saxon word, *scrobb*, a bush. In his *Herbal* of 1562 William Turner wrote: 'In the Southe countre a Crab tre, in the North countre a Scarb tre.' So the crab's habit of not reaching tree stature had been noticed. Or the name may derive from 'crabbed', indicating that it is a tree of 'awkward character' with its uneven branching and irregularly twisted boughs. It may even go back to the seashore crab, odd-angled and awkward.

ELM (*Ulmus spp*)

The tragic ravages of Dutch Elm Disease have recently centred attention on hedgerow elms, although these are but relics of former woodlands made up entirely of elms. The elm, however, seems to typify the British hedgerow tree; it is probably not as frequent as the oak, but it is one of the most imposing, its winter silhouette in field or hedgerow an integral part of much of our countryside. Today, although elm woodland still survives in one or two areas, most of it has been chopped down so that man can bring the land under the plough; elms thrive best where the soil is rich. It is in hedgerows that we have known

ELM

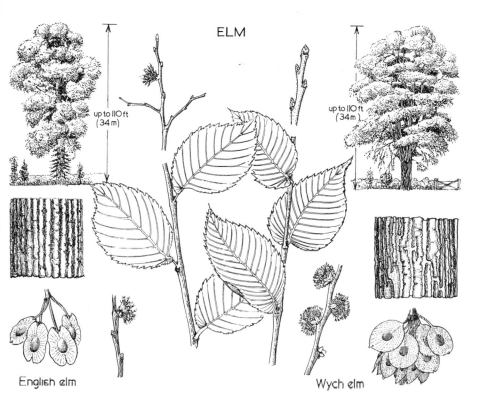

up to 110 ft
(34 m)

up to 110 ft
(34 m)

English elm

Wych elm

them in relatively large numbers. In areas where sandy soil predominates, on fens and heaths, in limestone and shallow chalk, the elm
is absent, and although some species have been recorded at a height of
more than 1,000ft (300m), they are generally confined to the lowlands.

The generic name, *Ulmus*, is of Latin derivation, but the tree was not
brought by the Romans. In fact the British name is the Anglo-Saxon
elm or *ulm*, and is frequently found in place names in this country and
in Germany. If elm is an 'introduced' species, it certainly came many
centuries ago. Some naturalists argue that it is a native British species.
The English and the smooth-leaved elm send out large numbers of
suckers, which might indeed be an adaptation to the British climate,
ensuring that although its seeds may not ripen in our weather, the
species will go on. In some years the elm does produce infertile seeds,

69

but this also occurs with other trees that produce seeds of small size and light weight. Much of the area around an elm tree is often grassy, and seeds falling nearby are not able to take hold. The suckers often succeed, especially when an elm is uprooted or cut down, sometimes eventually growing taller than the departed parent.

Three main species of elm occur in hedgerows in the British Isles: the wych elm (*Ulmus glabra*), the smooth-leaved elm (*U. carpinifolia*) and the English elm (*U. procera*). The wych elm is the commonest species in highland Britain, as its alternative names of 'mountain' and 'Scots' elm suggest. 'Wych' means 'pliant' and 'supple', but the tree may have derived its name from some of the items made from its timber. At one time it was used extensively to make wyches or whycches, chests used by writers; it was also used for making both pipes and troughs in which brine was carried from salt springs, known alternatively as wyches.

The leaves of the wych elm are larger than those of the English or the smooth-leaved species, and the wych does not sucker. An extremely large tree when it develops well, it will reach a height of 70 to 120ft (up to 40m), with a maximum girth of over 50ft (15m). When the tree is young the bark is distinctively grey and smooth; it becomes much rougher in appearance with age, and takes on a brown tinge. The long branches tend to curve upwards, ending in thick shoots. The leaves are arranged in a straight line along both sides of the twigs. Although oval in general outline, the midrib does not divide the leaf into equal parts, and so the shape is somewhat irregular, becoming broader towards the tip. Leaf margins are toothed, the surfaces rough, even harsh, a feature not shared by the common elm.

As with other species of elm, the deep purple-red flowers can be seen either late in February or early in March, appearing before the leaves have opened. Pollination is brought about by the wind. The fruit is produced later in the year; a pale green membrane-like structure covers the seed, the whole taking the form of an oblong samara, about an inch long, which is carried in the wind. The elm grows for around thirty years before it starts to produce seeds, and even after that good crops occur only every two or three years.

The female white-letter hairstreak butterfly will lay its eggs on the leaves of the wych elm, and the louse-shaped caterpillars can be seen feeding on the leaves in May or on the flowers earlier.

The grey-brown bark of the smooth-leaved elm is broken by deep indentations with long vertical fissures. A fully mature smooth-leaved elm may be more than 100ft (35m) in height, and over three hundred years old. Old elms can be dangerous because the branches become brittle and may break off in high winds; rot develops in the heartwood.

The leaves, about 3in (7.5cm) long, are basically elliptical in outline, light green with a long stalk. The flowers, as with other elm species, appear early in the year before the leaves are out, sometimes so profusely that the whole tree seems covered with a tinge of purple. The seeds, smaller than those of the other elms, appear later, borne on the twigs in large clusters; although many may be sterile, some will germinate in the following spring.

Quite frequently found in the eastern counties of the British Isles, the smooth-leaved elm is noted for prolific production of suckers. In some places whole hedges have grown up in this way, and it is possible to see a large elm flanked on either side by smaller trees diminishing in size the further they get from the parent.

With its greatest distribution in the Midlands, the English elm has dark-brown bark. The dark-green double-toothed leaves appear in April and, as with all the smooth-leaved variety, are about 3in long. Flowers appear earlier, in February or March, and the seeds borne singly in a circular membrane, are generally sterile. New trees are produced by suckers sent out by the parent elm. One of the problems with the identification of elms is that all species hybridise.

One investigator classified elms by using leaf shape, and from this managed to distinguish three species. However, these surveys were limited to elms in parish boundary hedges, because the investigator thought, almost certainly correctly, that these were likely to contain the oldest-established elms. As elms usually live no more than about 500 years, and parish boundary hedges may be over 1,000 years of age, his trees are unlikely to have been originals, though he considered that they were probably direct descendants, via suckers.

The smooth-leaved elm (*Ulmus carpinifolia*) probably first appeared here in Bronze and Iron Age periods. Certain settlements bear Anglo-Saxon place names derived from the tree, including Witcham, Elmdon and Elmswell: the first does not refer to a wych elm, but derives from differences in local dialect.

When large numbers of elms were destroyed in the recent prolonged outbreak of Dutch Elm Disease, the tree became national news. First noted in Holland (hence the name) in 1920, the disease spread rapidly through most European countries, and was recorded in England in 1927. In the early 1930s, in fact, the disease caused great concern, but gradually its spread slowed down and occurrences became fewer. Then a virulent epidemic began towards the end of the 1960s, reaching a peak towards the second half of the 1970s.

Dutch Elm Disease spreads fast in warm dry summers, and after those of 1975 and 1976 it reached new areas. The Forestry Commission has kept careful notes of its progress, and has recorded the distribution of the three major species of elm. Estimates made by various organisations suggest that at least 1,000 elms were being destroyed *each day* when the disease was at its worst.

One particular bark beetle, *Scolytus destructi*, nicknamed the 'elm destroyer', is held responsible for carrying the infection. It feeds and breeds below the bark of the elm tree, and carries with it the spores of the fungus *Cerotostomella ulmi* which causes the disease. During earlier outbreaks the beetle itself was mistakenly identified as the elm destroyer. The clue to its role came when the disease was noticed to be at its worst among elms growing near the larger ports: a new strain of the disease was found on rock log elms being imported from Toronto, Canada. Some live beetles from North America were discovered, and these were already known to carry the fungus on that continent.

The first sign that a tree is infected with Dutch Elm Disease is a yellowing of some of the leaves during summer. This will probably start on an isolated branch, where the beetle has landed with the fungus. Slowly, throughout the summer and autumn, the yellowing spreads. Sometimes it will only infect and kill one particular part of the tree; more often, however, the whole tree will eventually die. This disease is still destroying thousands of trees throughout the British Isles; it has at least drawn attention to the fact that trees in general, not only elms, are disappearing from the country scene at alarming speed.

The elm tree has been known as *elven*, believed to be associated with elves. In Devon, if elm leaves fell prematurely then cattle disease would follow, and elm trees were supposedly never struck by lightning. Close by, in Cornwall, the maypole taken to the village on 30 April to be decorated for display on May Day was always made of elm.

Elm is a strong wood, and was often used for the dividing sections in cowsheds and stables, because it could withstand continual kicking from animal hooves. It has proved its worth for cattle cribs and mangers, and also for the hubs of wooden wheels—bent elm is extremely strong. Straight trunks and branches were often used for early water pipes, and some put underground in London in 1613 were still 'as good as new' when uncovered in 1930.

FIELD MAPLE (*Acer campestre*)
Like so many trees, maples have been cultivated and many different ones will be found in parks and gardens. Only three occur commonly in the countryside, and of these only the field maple, the small-leaved maple, is a native: it is also known as the English maple.

When fully grown the field maple may be 20 to 40ft (6 to 15m) tall. It may tower above the surrounding hedgerow vegetation, but often remains merely an inconspicuous shrubby bush often the result of coppicing in the past. Fully grown specimens have superb ornamental value in the countryside hedgerow. Occurring particularly frequently in south-east England, it is also found on lime-rich soils in the north and west. It does occur in Scotland but much less commonly.

The leaves vary widely in size, from 2 to 4in (5 to 10cm) across, the smallest on the little shrubby maples, the largest on the taller trees; kidney-shaped, they have between three and five lobes. By May the insignificant greenish-yellowish flowers appear on upright umbels.

Although 'perfect' flowers—containing both male and female parts —are usually produced, sometimes both perfect and male flowers, or alternatively just male ones, may occur on the same specimen. Like the sycamore, a near relative, the field maple produces paired winged seeds known as 'keys' or samaras—similar to ash seeds although more pendulous. In late summer the keys may take on gold or deep crimson hues, before ripening to brown.

73

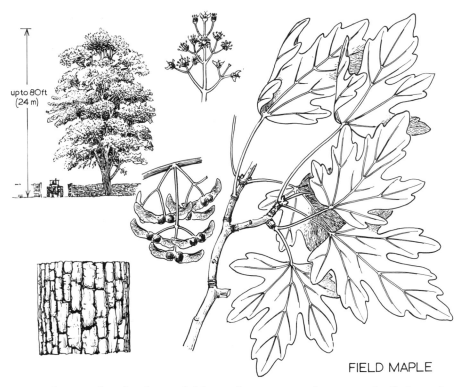

FIELD MAPLE

The trunk of a large field-maple tree may be around 2ft (60cm) thick. The light brown bark on a young tree has a rough, deeply networked, fissured surface; as growth continues the fissures tend to disappear, the bark becoming much smoother. In young trees the main bark on the trunk may flake off, and it often has a cork-like texture. Many of the young branches will also have somewhat spongy ribs, akin to those seen on elms. Young shoots have a grey, rather than brown, ground colour.

The timber is not especially valuable, though it is hard and fine-grained, and was used by cabinet workers. Country folk have fashioned it into fancy pipes and snuff-boxes. In Wales, the tree is called *masarn*: the old 'mazer', a wooden drinking bowl or goblet, was worked from maple wood. Welsh craftsmen have long chosen it for bowl and spoon making, and its fine texture comes up well when highly polished.

Wood taken from the root has particularly good grain markings. Turners use it for dishes, cups, trenchers, etc.: John Evelyn in 1664 wrote that the turner found it superior to beech for making dishes, cups and trays, and the joiner for tables or inlaying, choosing it particularly for the delicacy of the grain. Some turners worked it so that it became almost transparent. The wood was used centuries ago for making harps: a harp made from maple wood was unearthed when a Saxon barrow was excavated at Taplow in Berkshire. The famous Sutton Hoo treasure also revealed part of a Saxon maple harp. Carvings in maple (or in oak or hawthorn) can be seen in many thirteenth-century cathedrals and churches.

The tree has few enemies, but the leaves do attract the attention of a gall mite, *Eriophyes macrorhynchus cephalodes*. Where this has attacked the upper surface, the gall is evident because of the very small red raised 'lumps'. As many as five hundred may cover an upper leaf surface.

Field maple has many local names, including maplin tree, in Gloucestershire, oak in Somerset and Devon, dogwood in Yorkshire, Somerset and Nottinghamshire, and whistlewood in Scotland. The fruits too have their common local names, which include kitty-keys in Yorkshire and boots-and-shoes in Somerset.

HOLLY (*Ilex aquifolium*)

The holly is the only evergreen tree regularly found in hedgerows, and although when fully grown it may reach a height of 40 or 50ft (12 to 15m), it is usually no more than a tall bush. Growing widely over much of the British Isles, it is generally absent from northern Scotland.

The old name for the holly is *holm* which is found in place names: Holmsdale, at the southern foot of the Surrey chalk hills, was named many centuries ago, and within Holmsdale are the names Holmbury and Holmwood, indicating the frequent occurrence of the tree locally.

The leaves are well-known to everyone and left untouched by the wise. In fact, the holly has two types of leaves: low down on the tree, where likely to be attacked by browsing animals, are the fierce ones, spiked with twelve to fifteen sharp spines. Above a height of about 8 or 10ft (2 or 3m), they may lack these.

The well-known seventeenth-century diarist John Evelyn had a very

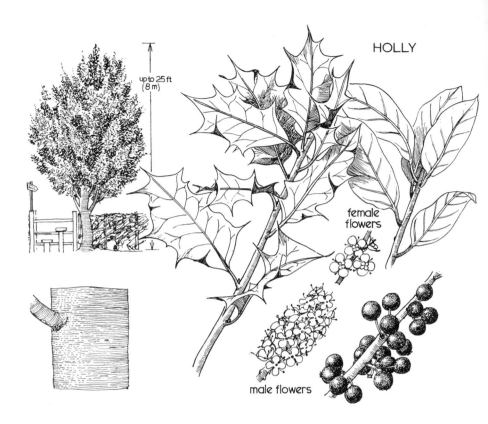

up to 25 ft
(8 m)

female
flowers

male flowers

good holly hedge, supposedly 10ft (3m) tall and 426ft long (130m) around his garden. In his *Sylva* is a fine description of it:

> Is there under heaven a more glorious and refreshing object of the kind, than an impregnable hedge of around four hundred feet in length, nine feet high, and five in diameter, which I can show in my now ruined gardens at Say's Court (thanks to the Czar of Muscovy) at any time of the year, glittering with its armed and varnished leaves? The taller standards at orderly distance, blushing with their natural coral. It mocks the rudest assaults of weather, beasts and hedge-breakers. . . .

The holly also had other uses. In earlier days, the young shoots were collected and dried to provide for winter food for cattle. Wild animals had probably already discovered its value before it evolved its protective spines.

Alternately arranged on the stem, the glossy-coated leaves have a hard, leathery, waxlike covering. They tend to be darker green on the upper surface than on the lower. But a lot of country people have never noticed the flowers of the holly. Appearing in May, these tiny, white but numerous blooms grow in small clusters. Although some trees have male and female flowers, many trees are single-sexed, and if a female tree has no male nearby, there will be no glossy, scarlet berries for hungry birds or Christmas decorations.

Early Christians took over the use of the holly from previous pagan rituals; they too believed that it would stop demons from entering homes or churches. Like several other trees, it was for a time supposed to have been the one from which Christ's cross was hacked. These symbolic links are related in the St Day Carol, performed by Cornish people, and are better recorded in the words of 'The Holly and the Ivy'. The spines represent the crown of thorns, the white flowers purity and the birth of Christ, the red berries drops of blood, and the bitter bark the passion.

Almost all parts of the holly have been used for healing purposes. The berries proved useful in small numbers as a purgative: taken in larger quantities they became an emetic. Leaves were used to cure fever, bringing down the temperature. More recently country folk took sprigs of holly to beat their chilblains—presumably the logic being that this would improve the circulation, but the cure must have been more painful than the complaint.

On large hollies, the smooth grey bark is often colonised by a lichen, *Graphis elegans*; the black fruiting bodies eventually appear as raised wedge-shaped patterns on the bark. Caterpillars of the holly blue butterfly (*Celastrina argiolus*) feed on the leaves of the tree in spring. The holly leaf-miner may completely cover the surface of the leaves in some seasons with a widespread network of tunnels. The dipterous parasite *Chromatomyia ilicis* may also feed from the leaves.

As the holly is not deciduous, its leaves fall and are replaced gradually throughout the year.

Holly wood has a hard, fine, white-grained texture, resulting from its slow growth; it has been used instead of boxwood for printing blocks as well as for engraving. It is sometimes dyed black and substituted for ebony. The timber is useful for small carvings, and has been made into chessmen and many other turned objects. Its whiteness contrasts effectively with the nearly black wood of the bog oak for inlays in furniture.

HORNBEAM (*Carpinus betulus*)

The hornbeam tree bears a superficial resemblance to the beech, but a closer look at the flowers, leaves and trunk soon dispels any doubt. Although it is not particularly common, its onetime reputed scarcity was almost certainly due to the fact that local people called it beech. The green bark has a smooth texture, although deeply fissured, and has a metallic-looking sheen to the surface. The tree reaches a maximum height of some 80ft (25m), but where soils are poor and dry it will never grow to this. It prefers low-lying, loam-rich soil or good clays.

As the name hornbeam may indicate, the wood is extremely hard or horny, the hardest of any of our native varieties. It was used for purposes for which metal is nowadays thought necessary, such as cogwheels; butchers' chopping-blocks and pulleys were made of hornbeam, and the name is even claimed to have come from the hornbeam yoke attached to the horns of bullocks when they were harnessed to the plough. Carpenters did not like working the wood, because its hardness quickly took the edge off their tools.

The leaves, appearing in May, later than beech leaves, are arranged alternately on the twigs. With a point and a serrated edge, they look like a cross between elm and beech leaves. The surface is rough, dark green and glossy, hairy on the underside. As autumn approaches, the leaves take on a pale yellow tinge, subtly changing to reddish-gold and ultimately to rust-brown. Some leaves fall in autumn but many may remain on the tree until spring.

The flowers appear with the leaves in May. Each tree bears both male and female catkins, cylinder-shaped and $1\frac{1}{2}$ to 2in (3.5 to 5cm) long. By autumn the ribbed fruit, about $\frac{1}{4}$in (6mm) long, appears. The winged seeds hang from the underside of the branches in sprays.

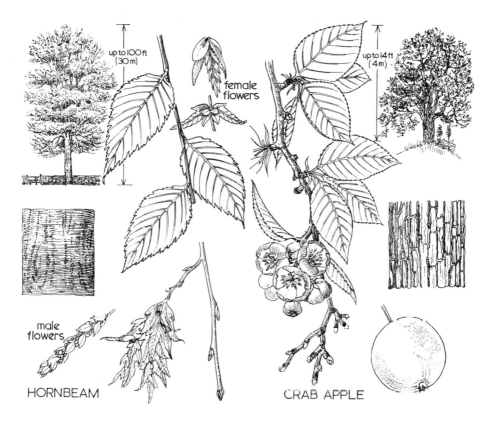

up to 100 ft
(30 m)

female
flowers

up to 14 ft
(4 m)

male
flowers

HORNBEAM

CRAB APPLE

The hornbeam is often considered a native species, but some trees have been brought in from overseas at various times; several were imported into Britain in the fifteenth century. Where it occurs north of a line from, roughly, Norfolk to Worcestershire, it has probably been planted. As a hedgerow tree it does well, not being attacked by cattle, and being very resilient when chopped back. At one time it was planted in formal gardens, particularly during the sixteenth and seventeenth centuries, where it would form both stately hedges and dense pleached alleys. William Morris's poem 'Shameful Death,' recording the murder of Lord Haigh, refers to the mysterious, stubborn quality of the hornbeam, with its masses of branches:

He did not strike one blow,
For the recreants came behind
In a place where the hornbeam grows,
A path right hard to find
For the hornbeam boughs swing so
That the twilight makes it blind.

OAK (*Quercus spp*)

For centuries the oak has been famed for its importance to man, particularly when it was used as timber for ships—the British 'hearts of oak'. In his *Sylva, or a Discourse on Forest Trees*, John Evelyn expressed concern about the fate of the English oak, in case, as he put it, a shortage should cause our 'wooden walls', our navy, to decrease in strength. The oak is still considered to be *the* British tree.

In Britain there are two species of wild oak: *Quercus robur*, English oak (the pedunculate oak), and *Quercus petraea*, the sessile oak. On the former the acorn cups have stalks, on the latter they are stalkless. Hybrids of the two are quite common. The natural oak woods of the British Isles have mostly disappeared, and the present plantations date from recent times, although large numbers of oaks still occur in hedgerows.

Large oaks have massive, sturdy, almost inpenetrable trunks, rising to a broad outline at the crown, formed by the wide spread and upward sweep of the limbs. The smallest fully grown oak will be around 60ft (18m), and although sturdy will bear no comparison to a big one, which may reach a height of 130ft (40m). Those found in hedgerows, are never as tall as the forest trees, which have been drawn upwards, and their girth may be a mere 4ft (1.2m) or so, as compared with the 10ft (3m) average of large specimens; 30ft (9m) or more is not unknown.

The pale-grey bark, thick and deeply fissured, provides a suitable refuge, albeit usually temporary, for all manner of insects. The branches are seldom straight, often growing in twisting, zigzag fashion. This characteristic proved of value to the early boat-builders, because natural bends could be used, eliminating the need to create a curve. In carpentry terms these bends are known as 'knees', and it is the trees

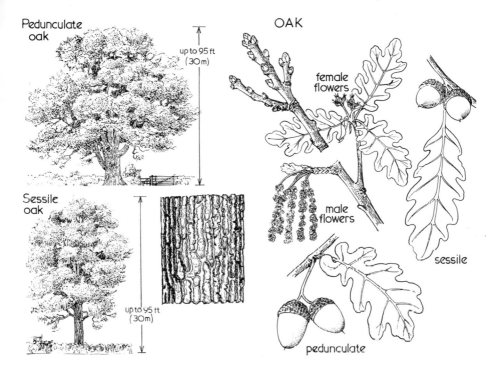

Pedunculate
oak

up to 95 ft
(30m)

Sessile
oak

up to 95 ft
(30m)

OAK

female
flowers

male
flowers

sessile

pedunculate

growing in hedgerows that seem to provide the boat-builder with the best knees. Veteran oaks can be seen at their best in the Midlands of England. In earlier days oaks were often pollarded, and these specimens lived longer; the effect of pollarding shows in the stoutness of the bole.

The oak flowers from April to May, the male flowers, green and inconspicuous, being borne in clusters along a suspended stalk. The fewer female flowers are held upright on short stems above the male catkins. Like other dull-coloured flowers, they depend on wind for pollination. The word acorn is derived from the Danish *korn*, oak seed. It is the overlapping scales at the base of the female flower that later form the cup that holds the acorn until it is ready to fall from the tree.

The leaves start to unfold in the middle of April, though some trees are habitually in full leaf in the middle of March every year, almost without fail. By late October the leaves start to change colour, most to a rich brown, others to a more delicate but striking orange-brown.

81

Colour change goes on into late November, although green leaves may sometimes be seen in December.

The name oak is derived from the Anglo-Saxon *ac*, and throughout the British Isles there are local variations. In the New Forest the tree is known as *yuk*; in Scotland as *ark*; *yak* in Hampshire; *woke* in the south-western parts of Britain. In Wales it is *derw*, the Gaelic variation being *darach* or *dair*, and it is the latter which is found in such local names as the derrys in Ireland.

Perhaps one of the most striking insects associated with the hospitable oak is the stag beetle (*Lucanus cervus*). On warm evenings in the southern parts of the British Isles, the insect will often be seen flying around oak trees. Its large jaws make it look fiercely menacing, but it is generally harmless. The 'hornless' female of the species lays her eggs in decaying oak wood, and when the larvae hatch they feed on it. Once the adults emerge, the male searches amongst the foliage of the tree for a mate.

Galls are found on many species of trees and other plants, and the oak in particular is afflicted with a number of different ones. The best known is the round 'oak apple'. When young it is spongy in texture, with an uneven surface. Later this becomes smooth. Oak apples and leaves are by tradition worn on 29 May to honour King Charles II, who hid in an oak tree. The galls are caused by different species of gall wasp; the growth is the tree's reaction to 'attack' by the wasp, which pushes through the young tissues of the leaf so that it can lay its eggs inside. If there is a hole in the 'apple', then the grub has changed into a winged gall wasp and gone; if the gall is whole, then the grub is still inside, either feeding or re-forming in the chrysalis stage.

The other most common species of galls on oak trees are the artichoke gall, made by *Cynips gemmae*, the bullet gall of *Andricus kollari* and the spangle gall caused by *Neuroterus quercus baccarum*. The latter is the one which is common on the back of oak leaves.

Of all the trees in Britain the oak seems to be the most attacked by insects. Probably at least 500 different invertebrates use the bark, wood or leaves. So ferocious is the attack in certain years that by early summer many oaks have been almost completely defoliated, although they are resilient enough to produce a second crop of leaves. One species which is responsible for a great deal of damage is the mottled umber moth (*Erannis defoliaria*), although this does also feed on other trees. Often the tiny caterpillars can be seen dangling by silken threads from the twigs, and to find them in your hair after walking beneath is common enough.

It is to be expected that a tree of the oak's status, one formerly so important to the British way of life, should feature strongly in folklore. Innumerable superstitions and beliefs attached to it—such as the old weather forecast that

> If the oak's before the ash
> You will only get a splash,
> If the ash before the oak
> You are sure to get a soak.

SPINDLE (*Euonymus europaeus*)
More abundant in the south-eastern counties of England than else-where, although widely distributed over much of England and Wales, the spindle may grow as a tree or, in hedges, as a straggly shrub. It favours lime-rich soils. As a mature tree it may reach up to around 20ft (6m); as a shrub or bush, it will reach 10–13ft (3–4m).

People tend to confuse the spindle with dogwood and buckthorn. Its distinguishing feature is its four-angled twigs. In spring, around May or June, it is bedecked with sprays of flowers, greenish-whitish, four-petalled and not the easiest to see, being camouflaged against the green foliage.

The shiny leaves may be either fan or egg shaped, and in autumn go through a series of colour changes from pale yellow to a final beautiful deep red. If crushed, the leaves give off an unpleasant smell.

By October there is no mistaking the spindle tree, for the distinctive bright pink four-lobed seed cases appear, cradling the orange seeds, as brilliant as rose hips, haws and bryony berries; the 'fruit which in our winter woodland looks a flower' (Tennyson, 'A Dedication').

In the past the tree played an important part in country life; its name goes back to the time when its rough, hard wood was used for spindle-making. At one time almost every woman had her own spindle.

83

SPINDLE

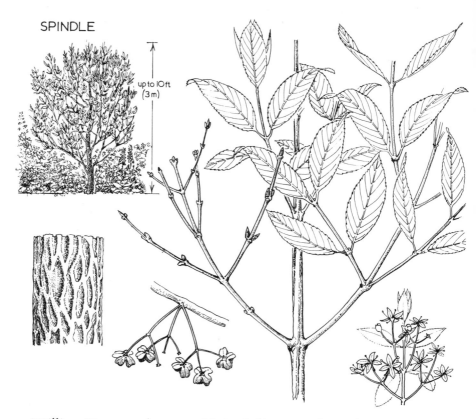

up to 10ft
(3m)

William Turner, who wrote his *Herbal* in 1586, claimed to have named it himself.

> I have sene this tree oft tymes between Ware and Barkwaye, yet al that I coulde never learn an English name for it, the Duche men call it Netherlande Spilboome, that is Spindel tree, because they used to make spindels out of it in that countrey, and me thynke it may be so wel named in English.

Local names include skewerwood and pegwood in Devon, spindlewood in Gloucestershire. Gypsies did use it for making skewers and pegs because of the hardness of its grain. It was also used at times for keys for the virginals, for toothpicks and viola bows. Gatter-tree and gatteridge are names meaning 'goat-bush', recording the belief that either the leaves or the fruit would poison goats. Flowers and bark were also considered to be poisonous; so strong was the belief in the spindle tree's lethal qualities in Buckinghamshire that it was given the name 'death-alder' and kept away from houses.

The smooth grey bark, which does contain a mild poison, is the only North European species of bark to contain gutta-percha, a tough greyish-black gum-like substance.

The fruits of the tree have several local names—in Gloucestershire 'louse berries'. Long ago they were collected in autumn, dried in the oven and then ground up into powder. This was then used to kill head lice, being sprinkled into the hair of young boys in particular to rid them of unwelcome visitors. Although the berries may have ill-effects on sheep and goats, they were used as a purgative, and Gerard, in his *Herbal*, recommended doses of three or four berries for this purpose.

Young shoots make a very good fine charcoal, formerly much sought after by artists.

One of the reasons why the tree seems to have vanished from many hedgerows in parts of the countryside is that it is the winter host-plant of the blackbean aphis (*Aphis fabae*). Since this has become a serious pest in areas where beans are an important crop, farmers have destroyed the tree. The ermine moth often lays its eggs in spindle where available.

WAYFARING TREE (*Viburnum lantana*)

As a shrubby feature of hedgerows bordering country roads, the wayfaring tree was once commoner than today, to judge from the comments of earlier writers. John Gerard remarked in 1597 on how often the tree was seen in thickets, as well as along hedgerows, bordering the drove roads of his day. It was found particularly along the tracks over the chalk downlands between London and Winchester, which Gerard knew well.

Drove roads were used as an alternative to turnpike roads, where tolls were charged. They came into their own especially around 1750 to 1850, constantly trampled by herds of cattle and flocks of sheep being driven from the fields to town markets to be sold. These wide

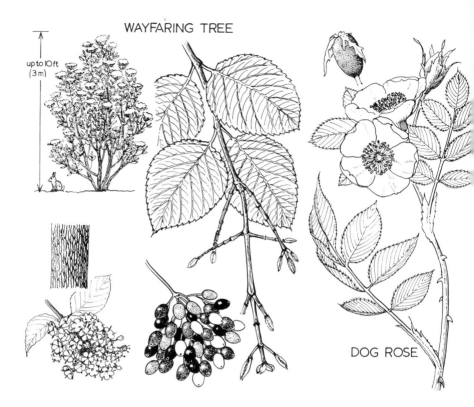

WAYFARING TREE

up to 10 ft
(3 m)

DOG ROSE

tracks, bordered on either side by wide indefinite verges, brightened
by a variety of wild flowers with tall hedges for a backcloth, were in
reasonable weather much kinder to the feet of man and beast than the
compacted turnpikes.

Gerard used the name *wayfaring tree* or *wayfaringman's tree*, and some
suggest that he took the word 'viorna' to be something which was an
'ornament' along the way—hence the meaning 'via' or 'wayfaring'.
Today the tree has many local names, including cotton tree, white-
wood, coventree and mealy tree, all recording the thick covering of
fine white hairs found on both young shoots and leaves. In other parts
of the country the wood was known as lithe-wort, whipcrop and
twistwood: craftsmen used the long, straight, strong shoots for
fashioning into whip handles, and as binding material for bunches of

vegetables or sticks. Three-year-old wood was used for stems for tobacco pipes.

The stubby black buds of the wayfaring tree are protected from the winter weather by a coat of rough hairs. The broad, wrinkled, heart-shaped leaves have a powdery appearance because of the hairs. With blunt tips and serrated edges they are 3 to 4in (7.5 to 10cm) long. The stems, also hairy, are slim with much branching, the shoots springing in pairs from each side of the stem.

The five-petalled white flowers, borne above the leaves in flat-topped clusters, 'coronets and fragrant snow' according to the poet William Howitt, appear in May and June. Once pollinated, they will form the bunches of fruits in autumn. These are oval rather than round, green at first, changing to various hues of yellow, coral and red and finally ripening to black. They are sour both to smell and to taste, and, if plentiful supplies of other berries are available around the hedgerow, birds will often pass them over.

Like so many wayside plants in earlier times, the wayfaring tree was used for its medicinal qualities. Both leaves and berries have been used as an 'antacid' for settling stomach upsets. Some country people prized it as a gargle, and even for fastening teeth. The leaves were taken and boiled to extract a black dye used as a hair-colourant.

Although the wayfaring tree most often grows in chalk and lime-stone country, it is also found in other areas, and along the south coast of Britain it grows on sandy soils. On downland, if left alone by sheep and rabbits, it spreads over quite large areas. In other places as far north as Yorkshire it will grow where the soils are dry. It is on the dry chalk that it reaches its greatest proportions, but its maximum is never more than 20ft (7m).

Hedgerow Shrubs

BLACKTHORN (*Prunus spinosa*)
Blackthorn (or sloe) has been extensively planted for hedges, although not as frequently as hawthorn except in a few parts of the country such as Cornwall. The stems grow in all directions and are liberally endowed with sharp thorns, characteristics which make the plant extremely

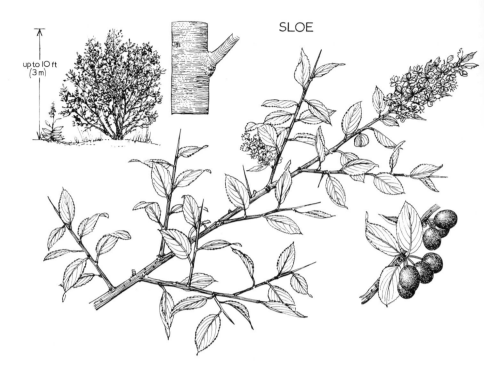

up to 10 ft
(3 m)

valuable as a hedging species, forming a virtually impenetrable barrier. Dead branches and stems of blackthorn are sometimes used in hedges as durable fillers.

The lovely snow-white blossom generally appears in March or April, before that of the hawthorn, and before the leaves are out. It contrasts spectacularly with the stark black bark. Bees are usually responsible for pollination, and then the familiar purple-black sloe, the wild plum, starts to develop. About $\frac{1}{2}$ in (12mm) in diameter, the fruit is held upright on its own short stalk. Although it is really black, its surface is shrouded beneath a delicate but nevertheless observable bloom which gives the skin a purple sheen. It has an intensely bitter taste before it ripens, setting the teeth on edge, though this does mellow later. When the surface skin starts to wrinkle, country people know that the sloe is ready to eat, and some collect it to make wine or sloe gin. (In a prolific year large quantities have been collected to make port!) Try filling a bottle one-third full of washed sloes pricked over with a fork, one-third full of sugar and one-third full of gin. Add two or three crushed sloe kernels and leave for a few months.

The Latin name of the blackthorn means 'spiny plum' ,and it is from this wild species that our modern cultivated plums have been bred. The black wood will make strong walking sticks, although it has few other uses. In Ireland the famous cudgel, the shillelagh, was carved from the wood of the blackthorn, and in earlier days in Britain too it was used for cudgels. As a common traditional feature of the country-side it has been celebrated by poets, including Edward Thompson ('Barren Sloe') and R. C. Ormerod ('Blackthorn in May'). In Scotland it is known as slae or bullister.

Like many other species of plants, blackthorn has religious conno-tations, both in the West Midlands and along the Welsh borders. A superstition that the stems should not be taken into the house is still believed in many parts of England. If a flowering branch of blackthorn was brought into a cottage it foretold death. In Worcestershire black-thorn branches were baked in an oven and then burned in the local cornfield, the resulting ashes being scattered over the earliest-sown wheat to ensure a good harvest. On New Year's Day in Herefordshire, a wreath made from blackthorn branches was charred in a fire then used as a decoration to be hung up with the mistletoe.

According to tradition, it was from the blackthorn that Christ's crown of thorns was made, and it bloomed at midnight on Old Christmas Eve. Even today in certain parts a period of cold weather known as blackthorn hatch or blackthorn winter is said to follow the period of warm weather responsible for bringing out the blossom.

DOGWOOD (*Thelycrania sanguinea*)
As one would suspect, dogwood has nothing to do with dogs. It is one of those names which has changed over the years as language has altered. Originally the wood from the tree was used for dags, skewers and goads, and from the first of these it took its name. The Latin *Cornus*, by which it was earlier known, correctly indicated that the wood was hard and tough, and it has also been used in turnery and for the handles of a wide variety of tools.

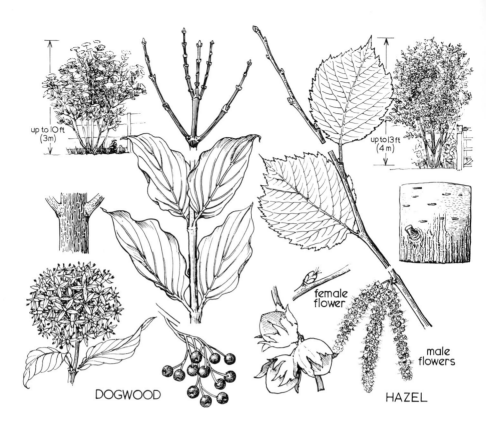

up to 10ft
(3m)

up to 13ft
(4m)

female
flower

male
flowers

DOGWOOD

HAZEL

Occurring in many hedgerows, dogwood is often mistaken for privet. A shrub by nature, it reaches a maximum height of no more than 6½ to 8ft (2 to 2.5m). Although it grows particularly well on chalk and lime soils, it is found over a wide area of Britain, as far north as the Scottish Highlands.

Its leaves are among the first seen in spring, appearing in March, pale green, oval and just under 1½in (4cm) long. Growing from opposite sides of the twigs, they are smooth on both sides, the twigs have a blood-red pigment; in autumn they turn to a very deep shade of red. The small white four-petalled flowers appear on the ends of the branches in late June or early July. Filled with nectar, but also having an unpleasant smell, they seem to attract a large number of insects to each flower cluster, including many small beetles and a variety of small flies. So dense is the insect cover at times it is difficult to see the flowers underneath!

Once the flowers die away, small green berries appear. They ripen slowly, and by September have a purple-black shiny skin. The outer fleshy covering has an extremely bitter taste; once the softer parts have been removed, there are two seeds inside. At one time an oil was extracted from the berries in France to be used for making soap and also in lamps.

Where there is very little competition in hedgerows, the suckers will quickly become established, and new dogwood plants will grow up at regular intervals.

The caterpillar of one of the commoner species of our British hairstreak butterflies, the green hairstreak (*Callophrys rubi*), will be found feeding on the dogwood, one of its main food plants.

The shrub has a variety of names, many including the word 'dog'; these others too reflect the uses made of the timber, skewerwood and skivertimber being examples.

Probably because of its unpleasant smell and the useless black fruits, over the centuries dogwood has attracted a bad name. Parkinson referred to it in his *Theatrum botanicum* (1640), as the 'dogge berry' tree: 'it was called this because the berries are not fit to be eaten, or to be given to a dog'. John Evelyn commended the wood for its hard texture, and suggested that it could be used for wedges, spikes and millcogs.

ELDER (*Sambucus nigra*)

Elder is quite a useful plant in hedgerows, usually growing as a low, bushy shrub. In favourable soil, such as a good loam, it can reach as much as 20ft (7m). its ultimate height is generally less than that of most other hedgerow trees. Moisture is essential to the plant for good growth. During the early stages of its life it grows with spectacular speed, perhaps more quickly than any other hedgerow shrub; plant a small piece of living elder, and see it take root and develop into a small shrub in what seems like no time at all. This is one of the reasons why it has often been specifically planted: it soon forms a reasonably thick barrier. Farmers would often break off small pieces to plant ready for filling gaps in hedgerows.

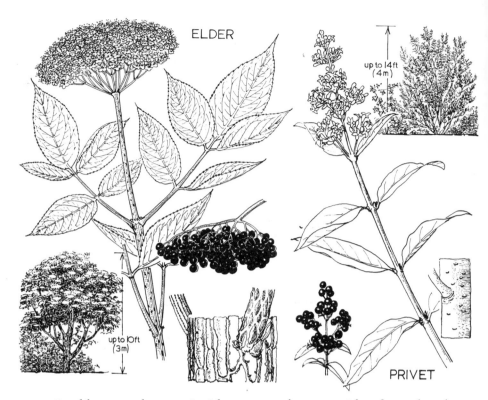

ELDER

up to 14ft
(4m)

up to 10ft
(3m)

PRIVET

In older trees the stem is either grey or brown, with a fissured cork-like texture; the surface may be covered with a thin coat of fine moss. In the annual twigs the bark is green, and has a rather peculiar, and to some people unpleasant, smell. In old, well-established specimens, the yellow-white wood takes on a hard, heavy appearance, and at this stage it has sometimes been used as a substitute for box. Its main uses appear to have been for tool handles and wooden spoons.

The leaves are arranged opposite each other on the twigs, and are made up of five, seven or nine leaflets with toothed margins. In autumn they change to a combination of rich golds, yellows and purple-reds; they may fall, but sometimes stay on the tree all the year round.

The large flat-topped sprays of sweet-smelling, whitish-creamy-yellow flowers appear in June. The individual flowers on the head are around a quarter-inch across. Although most country-folk like their scent, some find it unpleasant. Elder scent attracts a large number of invertebrates, and flies in particular tend to congregate on the platform-like flower heads. Once the flowers have faded, the familiar small round drupes—elderberries—appear; green and small at first, they ultimately take on a purple-black sheen, hanging in large clusters, avidly collected by the home winemaker in the autumn. Earlier in the year he might have gathered some of the white flowers: sometimes these are used for winemaking, sometimes for other culinary purposes, such as to flavour gooseberry jam. There is no doubting when the local birds have eaten the berries, purple stains appearing in their droppings scattered far and wide from the source of the food! To humans, although pleasant enough added to stewed apple, they have an insipid taste on their own; they have for generations, however, been prized for home winemaking.

The pithy inside is easily removed from elder twigs, leaving an outside tube which has been used for many thousands of years for a variety of purposes. It is known, for example, that the Greek gods called it *sambuke* (compare its Latin name, *Sambucus nigra*), and the wood was used for musical instruments. Names given to the elder in the north of England indicate that the easy removal of the pith was considered its main point of interest: it is called boretree, bottery (probably a corruption of the latter) and bourtree. The hollowed stems were even used for pop-guns—Shakespeare referred to 'a perilous shot out of the elder gun'.

In local superstition, the tree is considered unlucky if taken into the house. When hedgers were collecting faggots to take home to burn, they always refrained from taking elder. In Lincolnshire if it was allowed into the house the devil would come in with it, whilst in Shropshire certain death would come to one of the family if the twigs were used for fuel.

According to one story, where elder was used to make the rocker on a child's cradle, the tree spirit would attack the child. A particular child was apparently punched black and blue in an unwarranted attack by the evil spirit, but as soon as the elder rocker was replaced with one of ash, the child's bruises disappeared. If an elder tree was cut down and used to make furniture, the elder mother inhabiting the tree would accompany the furniture, with the result that it broke, persistently squeaked, or warped! Farmers were loath to use elder switches for cattle-driving. Scottish border tradition has it that the elder only grows where blood has been spilt on the ground.

In some parts of the country, on the other hand, the elder was planted in gardens because people believed that it would ward off witches. Branches of it were sometimes placed near a grave to protect the body from lurking evil spirits. According to a story from Waddesdon in Buckinghamshire, early in the 1900s a young girl had a large number of warts on her hands. A neighbour counted the warts, and then went out and cut the same number of notches in an elder twig, eventually burying the twig in the ground. The stick slowly decomposed, and as it did so the warts gradually disappeared from the girl's hands.

According to an old country saying from Sussex,

> An eldern stake and blackthorn ether
> Will make a hedge last forever.

The local 'blackthorn ether' was the wound made where the flexible underwood was cut on the major stakes when a hedge was being layered.

In spite of the awe in which elder was held, in some areas it also had many uses. If the leaves were picked on May Eve they were, we are told, a sure cure for toothache, bites from mad dogs, melancholy and the wounds inflicted by adders. Elder leaves hung in the house would keep flies at bay, and if a horse-rider carried an elder twig in each pocket he would never suffer from saddle-soreness. Writing in 1722, Christopher Gullet remarked that if the elder was used to 'whip' cabbages, turnips and fruit trees, then any blight attacking them would disappear. The famous Roman historian Pliny remarked that elder was very good for whistle-making, and that the most resonant notes came from twigs which grew out of earshot of the cock-crow.

The pith is extracted and used by botanists for holding leaves and stems while they cut their sections for use under the microscope—

though nowadays technology has overtaken the humble elder tree, and polystyrene 'pith' is often used instead. The natural pith is also used by scientific-instrument makers, and watchmakers have used it for removing dust and grime from delicate mechanisms.

Piers Plowman used the name 'eller' for the tree, and this is still current today in Cheshire, Kent, Lincolnshire and parts of East Yorkshire, as well as in Sussex. Apparently the word comes from the Anglo-Saxon 'eller' or 'eldern', which is thought to mean 'kindler': when the pith was removed from the twigs, the hollowed-out tube could be used to blow-up a fire.

HAWTHORN (*Crataegus spp*)
Of all the shrubs used in hedging, the hawthorn is the commonest. The two species used are *Crataegus monogyna* and *Crataegus oxycanthoides*. They are much alike, and since the leaves of either show considerable variation in shape and character, the task of distinguishing between the two is something for the experts. *C. monogyna* is by far the more usual and is almost universally considered to be *the* hawthorn; it is widely distributed over much of the British Isles. The other species, *C. oxycanthoides*, is generally limited to clay soils and found mainly, though not exclusively, in woodlands; it is often known as the woodland hawthorn, and because it is commoner in the Midland counties also as the Midland hawthorn. It has probably become established in Midlands hedges as a result of the removal of large tracts of woodland where it once flourished.

The leaves of *C. monogyna* are usually quite deeply dissected; those of *C. oxycanthoides* generally less so. The leaves of the latter usually have a glossier sheen to the surface, and may be darker in colour.

There are differences in the make-up of the flower of the two species, the flower stalk of the common variety having a covering of hairs. The woodland species generally has two seeds inside the red 'haw', whereas *C. monogyna* only has one.

On *C. monogyna* the bark has a cracked surface, the splits forming almost irregular rectangles. In some trees it is orange-brown, in others pink-brown.

If allowed to grow as a tree, the hawthorn can reach a height of

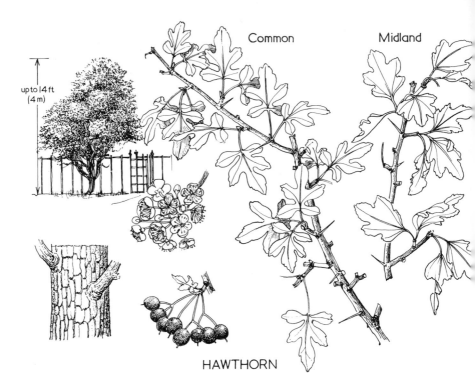

Common **Midland**

up to 14 ft
(4 m)

HAWTHORN

about 40ft (12m), its trunk around 4ft (1.2m) in circumference. During the first fifteen years of life, it will grow quite rapidly—one of its names is 'quickthorn'; after that it slows down, and may go on growing for more than 250 years. The hard, tough nature of the wood is indicated by the genus name, *Crataegus*, which derives from the Greek *Kratos*, strength.

The white flowers, bursting forth from the buds, are borne in bunches which may contain sixteen or more individuals. Opening around mid-May and known as 'may', they generally give off a pleasant scent, at least until the blossom has started to fade. The tinge of pink comes from the anthers in the centre of the petals. To look down from a hill on to a hawthorn-hedged landscape in May is an experience that fires many people's enthusiasm for the 'traditional' British hedge.

After pollination, the flowers faded and petals gone, the fruit will be developing and in autumn the bushes are covered so thickly with crimson haws that the leaves are almost hidden from view—valuable food for hedge residents and visitors. Underneath the fleshy exterior the actual seeds are protected so that when birds or mammals eat them they will not be digested but will be expelled with the droppings, ensuring the propagation of a new generation. Although large numbers of these seeds do germinate, many young plants are of course nibbled by grazing animals, and rabbits were—at least until the reduction in numbers due to myxomatosis, and still are in some places—responsible for keeping these shrubs at bay away from the hedge itself. The hawthorn is a valuable plant for wildlife: the larvae of some 180 species of moths feed on the leaves, twenty-five of these having no alternative food source.

The number of names used for the hawthorn in various parts of the country indicate its familiarity: may tree, bread-and-cheese tree (country children used to chew the newly emerged tender green leaves), whitehorn, peggles, hipperty-haw, tramps' supper, hawsey bush, moon flower and quickthorn are just a few. The mass of white and pink flowers heralds the start of what one can still hope will be a warm summer, the large clusters brightening and scenting hedgerows that at this time of the year, now the brilliant green of new leaves has dulled, are often drab.

Numerous sayings and legends are associated with the hawthorn; it was always an important plant to country people. The old axiom 'Don't cast a clout till May is out' refers to the fact that the flowering time of the shrub heralds a warmer period—it is not a reference to the end of the month of May! If hawthorn was planted next to a house, then the tree would ensure that the occupants were safe during even the severest thunderstorms, because it would ward off the lightning. Country people believed—still do believe in some areas—that it was unlucky to bring may blossom into the house. The little folk were associated with the bush in Ireland: where a lone hawthorn stood on the side of a hill it was known as a 'shiggy', having been planted by the little people. No one dared remove the tree, for they knew that the little people would wreak vengeance.

Hawthorn also has associations with ancient fertility rites. The tree flowered during the 'breeding' season, when new life was appearing in the countryside. In Christian folklore, the hawthorn staff which Joseph of Arimathea pushed into the ground at Glastonbury, Somerset, took root and grew. This variety of *C. monogyna* is also known as Glastonbury hawthorn. Apparently, so the story goes, Joseph's staff took root, and perpetuated the species which burst into bloom at Christmas. A bush said to have sprung from the original one grows in the grounds of Glastonbury Abbey today.

To plant the hedgerows which the enclosures demanded, the production of young hawthorn plants was an important part of the work on estates about 150 years ago. The seeds were collected about eighteen months before they would be sown, mixed with sand and stored in a 'rotting pit' in the ground. The seeds were planted in spring, and when two years old the seedlings were transplanted. At four years they were planted along the line of the desired hedges.

For the first few years after planting the young hawthorns had to be carefully weeded, and if the hedge was growing too tall and straggly it was trimmed with a bill-hook. Once the hawthorns grew to over 6ft (about 2m), they had to be 'managed', and were cut and laid. This was a particularly important craft (see page 193), because the hedges needed to be stock-proof. It is now dying out in some areas but is still practised vigorously in certain parts of the country; for the uninitiated it is fascinating to watch.

To keep a hedge in satisfactory stock-proof condition, it must be managed properly throughout its life, which is likely to be for more than one hundred years.

In some cases, a ditch was dug, the soil being thrown up to form a bank; hedge, ditch and bank all had to be carefully set on the farmer's own land if they were along the farm boundary.

Although four years old when planted as hedge 'markers', the hawthorns were still relatively small, and susceptible to trampling by farm stock. At this time wire was scarce, and expensive, and so miles and miles of either post-and-rail fencing or hurdling were erected on *both* sides of the new hedges. With the many thousands of miles of hedges being planted, the felling of trees made a drastic demand on the country's wooded areas, although at the same time it provided work

This hedge has been trimmed but not laid—it is not stockproof (*Goodman Photographics*)

for many thousands of men. The four-year-old hawthorn plants were placed 4in (10cm) apart, which meant that for every mile (or 1.6km) length of hedge being planted, there were no fewer than 16,000 hawthorns; and a mile of hedging could only enclose a square field of about 50 acres (over 20 hectares). So the number of seedlings raised must have been colossal.

HAZEL (*Corylus avellana*)

Few, if any, hazels ever reach tree height, the majority ending up as large shrubs. Older specimens may reach about 13ft (4m) in a hedge, and if left undisturbed may eventually reach about 19–20ft (6m). The bark is brown, shiny and peels. The young twigs are conspicuous, covered with numerous hairs. Alternate leaves, almost heart-shaped, have rounded tips. Appearing in May they stay on the tree until about November. When first opened they may have a purple hue, but this gradually disappears.

Perhaps the most conspicuous feature of the hazel are the catkins early in spring. These male catkins—often known as lambs'-tails—are already on the tree in the previous autumn, as small, greyish-greenish lumps. They grow slowly during the winter days, and are about 2in (5cm) long by February, rich with the pollen which gives them their distinctive yellowish colour. The spring winds swing the catkins, scattering the pollen which may land on and fertilize the female flowers. These are mere inconspicuous, swollen buds, occurring on the top ends of the tree's twigs. Their fine crimson threads are the reproductive organs to be dusted with pollen. The hazel-nuts ripen late in August or early in September; rich in oil, the nuts are valuable food for many animals.

One of the shrubs used for single-species hedges in the south-west of the British Isles is hazel, and it is also found in the south-east and in some areas of East Anglia. It was used in areas of older enclosures, but was not often chosen later and so is seldom encountered as a hedging species where the open-field system was used right up until the heyday of the enclosures, the seventeenth and eighteenth centuries.

The modern name 'hazel' has its roots in Anglo-Saxon. *Haesl* or *haesel* was a 'baton of authority'. The name was well-suited to the tree, for hazel rods were not only used to drive cattle, but in ancient times to drive, and no doubt to beat, errant slaves.

Like the hawthorn the hazel features in early folklore, probably because it was common especially around the old enclosures. The plant was—and still is—the choice of water diviners or dowsers, who were able to locate water with the hazel twig. If the divining rod was to be successful, it had to be cut on St John's Eve or Night. Using a forked twig, the diviner walked over the ground holding the two prongs of the hazel fork. When passing over water, the stick started to twitch and vibrate.

In Celtic times the tree was associated with both fertility and fire. Small hazel twigs kept in a house were supposed to protect it from lightning; kept on a boat, they would preserve people on board from shipwreck. The hazel rod was also used to 'find' thieves, until the sixteenth century.

A good crop of hazel-nuts was said, particularly in the Midlands, to foretell disasters: 'Many nuts, Many pits,' ran the old saying, the pits in this case referring to graves. However, a heavy crop of nuts in other parts of the country brought better things: plenty of hazel-nuts apparently meant plenty of babies. The philosophy behind this is not clear.

A Welsh tradition was that if hazel twigs were woven into hats, the wearers were bound to find their 'heart's desire'. If a double hazel-nut was carried around in the pocket, the lucky person would never suffer from toothache. On St Mark's Eve, during Hallowe'en, it was the custom to place a row of hazel-nuts on the hot embers of the fire, and each nut 'belonged' to one girl. She would utter the name of her favourite man. If the nut jumped then the match would be a successful one.

> If you love me, pop and fly
> If not, lie and die.

Animals could be protected by the hazel's magic powers. When a horse had eaten too much, hazel twigs were bound to make it well again, provided of course that the appropriate rhyme was recited. A breast band made from hazel and placed around a horse would prevent 'attacks' from fairies. If cows were lucky enough to chew hazel leaves then their milk yield was supposed to increase.

PRIVET (*Ligustrum vulgare*)
In hedgerows wild privet generally grows only to shrub-size, although in lime-rich soils it may eventually reach 19–20ft (6m). Its name may derive from the same root as 'private': the plant was used extensively for enclosing gardens and ensuring privacy. But as early as 1548 it was known as privet, from the old English *pryfet*, and probably the real origin of the word has been lost.

It has a number of local names. Some, like black tops and blue poison (Somerset), refer to the berries. In Cornwall it has become known as skedge, skidgery and skedgewith, names which come from Cornish words for 'shade tree'.

The lance-shaped, simple leaves, 1–2in (2.5–5cm) long, on short stalks, are opposite each other on the twigs; dark green above and lighter on the underside, they have a smooth, shiny surface. In autumn they turn to a light violet, and mostly falling from the shrub by the middle of winter, although some may remain on the branches, depending on weather conditions.

A smooth grey to brown bark clothes the tree, although in young branches the colour tends towards olive-green, with a sprinkling of hairs. If privet is left uncut, as it often is in hedgerows, in June or July according to situation it will produce pyramid-shaped sprays of creamy-white funnel-shaped, four-petalled flowers. Their sweet, heavy scent (to some people fishy and unpleasant) helps attract small insects which enter the funnels and pollinate them.

The fruits, small black, shiny berries, are fully ripe in September or October: though poisonous to man, they are liked by birds. The liquid used for boiling privet leaves was recommended for curing mouth and throat infections. At one time the fruits of the wild privet were collected for a crimson dye to be extracted. This was added to alum to form a deep green colour, which was used on silk.

ROSE (*Rosa spp*)
Several species of wild rose are commonly found in the hedgerow; three are quite widely distributed. Although they may grow as climbers, they can also support themselves as free-growing bushes. Dog rose (*Rosa canina*), downy rose (*R. villosa*) and the smaller sweet briar (*R. rubiginosa*), and also the field rose (*R. arvensis*), are frequently encountered, dog rose and sweet briar particuarly in the southern counties. Sweet briar, the least common, is Shakespeare's 'eglantine'.

The curved spines of the dog rose, although well spaced, offer the plant some protection from marauding animals. The leaves are compound, made up of two or three pairs of leaflets with serrated margins. The strikingly beautiful flowers usually appear in June, in clusters of between one and four blooms, sometimes more. These vary in colour from almost white to shades of pink and even deep red. Their sweet scent disappears once they are fully opened. The familiar fruits, the scarlet rose hips, grace miles of hedgerows in autumn, sought out by numerous species of birds.

In some parts of the country there are numerous variations on the dog rose, the commonest wild rose; no fewer than *sixty* micro-species have been recorded, with probably many others awaiting recording by the dedicated botanist. It occurs in both lowland and highland parts of the British Isles, though less often in Scotland, because it dislikes soggy or windswept situations. Frequently growing as a bush or shrub in its own right, when the need or opportunity arises it will take advantage of the other species growing in a hedge, using its large strong thorns to gain a grip on its surrounding neighbours and push its branches skywards.

So much admired are these plants in the countryside, and they must have been even more apparent in earlier days, that several legends have grown up around them. The best known is that a beautiful maiden was pursued by someone she did not love, and in order to elude him she turned into a rose plant, the spines ensuring that he could not get near her. Queen Alexandra, the wife of Edward VII, used the rose as an emblem for the 'flags' sold to collect money for the charities supported on Alexandra Rose Day.

Although the cultivated rose grown so widely in gardens for many centuries has been used as an antidote for all kinds of ills, only one part of the wild rose was allowed any value by the earlier herbalists. This was the 'robin's pincushion'. Many species of wild rose are attacked by *Diplolepis rosae*, a gall wasp: the female lays her eggs in the tissues of the plant, and as the grubs develop a bright-red gall forms, with a moss-like surface. The pincushion's correct name is bedeguar gall.

Known as 'briar balls' in bygone days, they were collected and sold to apothecaries to be dried, powdered and boiled. The resulting essence was drunk as a cure for colic, to disperse gallstones or to act as a diuretic. Nicholas Culpeper in *The English Physitian Enlarged*, published in 1669, suggested that white worms, parasitic to the larvae of *Diplolepis rosae*, should be dried and ground up, the powder then being mixed with liquid and drunk. This would kill and get rid of any worms in the human belly. Whole bedeguars were collected and hung around the neck as a protection from whooping cough.

7

Common Hedgerow Plants

COW PARSLEY (*Anthriscus sylvestris*)
Known also as wild chervil and beaked parsley, the cow parsley is one of the Umbelliferae, the small flowers being clustered together in umbels, or heads, rayed like the spokes of an umbrella. Of the hedgerow parsleys, this species is the first to flower, and in May nearly every hedgebank in the country becomes richer for its presence. Its flowers, creamy-white, soft and delicate in structure, are in keeping with the fine, lace-like nature of the leaves: Queen Anne's lace is an old name for it.

Below the soil a substantial tap root supports the hollow, slightly hairy stem which may rise to over 3ft (1m) above the ground. The fern-like leaves are covered with fine down. It is the shape of the seed, rather like a bird's beak, that has given the plant the alternative name of beaked parsley. The plant begins to develop from December onwards, its leaves being useful early food for animals working about the hedgerow.

Why should such a plant have been connected with the devil? Some of its earlier names are devil's meat, devil's meal, devil's parsley and devil's oatmeal. Even the enterprising herbalists could find few if any uses for it. Certainly cow parsley is not poisonous, though a number of other plants somewhat resembling it are. The leaves are sometimes collected by country people to feed to pet rabbits.

FOXGLOVE (*Digitalis purpurea*)
One of the best-known and most striking of our countryside flowers, one preferring shady hedgebanks, particularly on acid soils, the foxglove is well loved and well documented in local customs.

A tall, stately plant in good conditions, the foxglove may reach a height of 5 to 6ft (nearly 2m). It can be either biennial or perennial. During its first year the leaves, arranged in rosette formation, remain close to the ground. It is only in the second year that the downy stem starts to grow up. The stalked leaves growing out from the root are pointed and 6in (15cm) or more in length, their surface soft and downy, with very small wrinkles on the upper side. The under-surface is much rougher, and on the larger leaves a distinct network of veins stands out from the background.

Along the stem the leaves are much smaller. Towards the extremity, the large bell-shaped flowers, usually deep pinkish-purple in colour, are seen from June to September. They all hang on the same side of the stem, and the inside of each is lighter and spotted. Those at the bottom of the spike flower first. Variations in colour do occur.

GROUND IVY (*Glechoma hederacea*)
Related to the cultivated garden mint, not to ivy, the ground ivy is an early hedgerow species, liking shaded hedgebanks. Its scent is less strong than that of mint, and to many people not as pleasant.

Its square, hard, reddish stems trail amongst the other plants in the hedgebank, rooting at the nodes, the points where it sends up the paired, stalked leaves, which are kidney-shaped, rounding towards the leaf stalk. Although usually green, where the plant grows in direct sunlight they may have a slight purple tinge.

The purple to blue flowers appear in whorls around the stem, at any time from March to June. John Gerard, the herbalist, wrote in the sixteenth century that 'Amongst the leaves come forth the flowers, gaping like little hoods.'

The scented leaves were gathered in the spring and boiled to make a tea, claimed to be a tonic—some said it drove away the last remains of an unsavoury winter! 'Come buy my ground ivy' was a not unusual street cry.

HEDGE BEDSTRAW (*Galium mollugo*)
Though similar to cleavers, on closer examination hedge bedstraw will
be found to have a more delicate máke-up. Commonest on the upper
regions of grassy hedgebanks, particularly in southern Britain, it is a
perennial, its long, thin stems between 3 and 5ft (1 and 1.5m) in
length and much more pliable than those of cleavers. Nor does it have
the hooks characteristic of its close relative.

Its stem may be smooth or hairy, and is rough where side branches
leave the main stem. Because of its weak stem and lack of hooks it is
not able to climb up other hedgerow plants; it is a straggler, growing
against them for support rather than on them.

The leaves, which grow in whorls of six to eight, are oval, broader
than those of cleavers, but widely varied in shape and size. The edges
are rough, the tip pointed. The flowers, small, four-petalled and white,
grow in dense clusters at the end of branched stems. The seeds, black
and rough-surfaced, are not so prolifically produced as those of cleaver
plants.

The family name of Galium comes from the Greek word *gala*,
milk. At one time some of the Galiums were added to milk to make it
curdle and in cheese-making. Cows which eat the plant when it is in
flower are reputed to produce milk which will sour very quickly. The
mollugo is from the Latin *mollus*, soft, so distinguishing it from cleavers.

HEDGE PARSLEY (*Torilis japonica*)
Hedge parsley is the latest hedgerow umbellifer to flower. It comes out
at any time from July and continues through until September, after the
blooms of beaked parsley and rough chervil are over. It is as common
as the earlier species but less well-known, mainly because of its later
flowering. An annual plant, its tall stem is solid, unlike that of the other
umbelliferous species, the outside broken up by fine grooves. The
whole outer surface is covered with downward-growing hairs.

Two types of leaves are found on the plant: those lower down,
towards the base of the plant, are broken up into a number of lance-
shaped, lobed leaflets. The upper leaves, at the base of the branches of
the stem, are simpler and more slender than the lower ones, although
also deeply toothed.

The upright stem is branched, with a flower head at the terminal. The hedge parsley is a stiffer, wirier plant than cow parsley or rough chervil, but the main distinguishing feature which sets it apart is that its flowers are pinkish-purplish-white in colour. The oval fruits can be distinguished from those of the cow parsley by their hooked spines.

HEDGE WOUNDWORT (*Stachys sylvatica*)

Its British name correctly labels the hedge woundwort's habitat. It is often found along shady hedgebanks, but as the name *sylvatica* implies, it also occurs in woods. A member of the mint family, it has a strong or even, to some nostrils, repugnant smell, particularly evident if you squeeze the stem.

Growing to a maximum height of around 3ft (1m) the large, toothed, heart-shaped leaves have a soft surface, the upper side in particular covered with a soft yet slightly bristly hair. Looking similar to nettle leaves, they are 2in (about 6cm) in length. Growing in pairs from the stem on long stalks, the largest leaves are towards the base of the plant; the smallest near the apex.

The claret-coloured flowers grow in rings around the upper part of the stem, usually arranged in sixes, giving the impression of a flowering spike. (The Latin name *stachys* means 'spike'.)

Woundwort was indeed used to treat cuts and abrasions, sometimes in a poultice. It is recorded that a farm labourer who cut a deep gash into his leg with his scythe applied hedge woundwort and in less than a week found his wound was completely healed. Relatively recent research substantiates the plant's reputation for healing properties, since an oil with an antiseptic quality has been extracted from the leaves.

JACK-BY-THE-HEDGE (*Alliaria petiolata*)

Usually found on the shaded side of hedgebanks, Jack-by-the-hedge is also known as garlic mustard or hedge garlic. In earlier times it was collected and used as a sauce—hence its earlier name of sauce-alone. It was thought particularly suited to fish dishes.

One of the commoner species along hedgerows and hedgebanks, it is widely distributed over England, less frequent in northern and western Scotland.

A tall, erect annual, its leaves are attached to the stem by long stalks. The leaves are either heart-shaped, with rounded teeth, or triangular with pointed teeth. They can be seen throughout the winter, although the stem does not start to grow until spring. Their 'offensive' smell is sometimes mentioned: when bruised they certainly smell like garlic.

The small, white, four-petalled flowers, appearing in May and June, attract midges as pollinating agents, though if no midges are around the flowers will self-pollinate successfully. The seed pods, about 2in (6cm) long, may be eaten by the caterpillar of the orange-tip butterfly (*Anthocharis cardamines*) in June, though the colour of the caterpillars is so closely akin to that of the seed pod that they remain almost invisible.

LESSER CELANDINE (*Ranunculus ficaria*)
Common in woodland, the lesser celandine (or pilewort) is also frequent in dampish and shady hedgerows. A member of the buttercup family, it is one of the very earliest of the spring flowers, its blooms 'brilliant, burnished gold stars'. 'Do you like butter?' the children will ask, holding a flower near your chin to see how much reflection from the petals shows on your skin.

Under the ground the roots give rise to large numbers of tubers, each of which will grow a new plant in favourable conditions. Like so many of the other early low-growing species, it traps the sunlight with its leaves to produce food before other larger species can obliterate it.

The leaves vary, those growing up from the root being smooth, shiny and generally heart-shaped, with wavy edges, held up on long stems. Sometimes the leaf surface is broken by black, white or even purple-brown blotches and patches. The majority of the smaller leaves are ivy-shaped.

It is those early golden flowers, starting to appear in February, that have captured the imagination of country folk for many centuries: Wordsworth wrote a poem specifically for 'The Lesser Celandine':

> There is a flower, the lesser celandine,
> That shrinks, like many more, from cold and rain,
> And, the first moment that the sun doth shine,
> Bright as the sun himself, 'tis out again.

William Turner left the first written record of the lesser celandine in 1548, describing it as the 'figwurt which groweth under the shaddowes of ashe trees'. It was commonly known as figwort or pilewort: the former for the fig-like nature of its roots, the latter because it was used as a 'cure' for piles. In several places, including Kent, and particularly in the nineteenth century, children used to collect lesser-celandine leaves to rub on their teeth to whiten them. Earlier it was thought that the tubers looked like cow udders, and they were collected and hung in the cow-shed to increase the cream content of the milk.

PRIMROSE (*Primula vulgaris*)
Although a typical woodland plant, the well loved primrose is also commonly found growing on hedgebanks. Like many other small species it flowers early and avails itself of the sunlight before being shrouded by more dominating hedgerow herbs. Odd flowers may be found in mild weather at almost any time of year. Reappearing in the same spot year after year, if it remains undisturbed, it has a thick rootstock under the ground.

The low-growing rosette of soft and wrinkled leaves protects the flower buds, usually growing singly on a slender pink stem, sometimes several to the stem. Two types of the delicate, pale yellow sweet-scented flowers occur: thrum-eyed and pin-eyed. The flower of the thrum-eyed variety has a short style, which ends about halfway up the corolla tube, the stamens being in a cluster around the top of the flower. In the pin-eyed species the style is longer, and the stigma, with its close resemblance to a pin head, can be seen near the top of the corolla tube, the stamens below this.

Among the many people to celebrate the primrose are Shakespeare, Milton, Burns and Cowper. Shakespeare observed the early appearance of the flowers, when few insects are around, and in *The Winter's Tale* commented on the 'pale primroses that die unmarried'.

The flower gets its name from the Latin *prima rose*, 'first rose' of the year. The Earl of Beaconsfield, Benjamin Disraeli, was particularly addicted to them and was said to be responsible for their decreasing numbers in his local Buckinghamshire countryside; the Conservative

Party formed the Primrose League, for the maintenance of Conservative principles, in his memory.

Since the primrose is so common in many areas, and so much loved, it is not surprising that it features in many country superstitions. In Sussex and parts of East Suffolk, when collecting the first posy of primroses in spring to adorn the house, at least thirteen flowers had to be brought in: if fewer were gathered then it bode ill for the number of eggs the household hen would hatch. Like so many other plants, primroses have been seen as a protection from witches: in the Isle of Man, a bunch of primroses was placed on the cow-shed floor on May Day, when the witches were at their most active!

RED CAMPION (*Melandrium rubrum*)
An extremely common plant along shady hedgebanks, where the soil is always moist, the red campion prefers calcareous soils.

First flowering in May, red campion usually blooms throughout the summer, sometimes until September. The clusters of rose-red flowers brighten up many an otherwise dull hedgebank. Each of the flower's five petals are so deeply notched that they are almost divided into two; they grow out from the stalk on slightly hairy stems. Male and female flowers are to be found on separate plants and so insects are needed to transfer the pollen from male to female. After pollination the calyx gradually increases in size to form an egg-shaped capsule. This ultimately opens to set free the ripened seeds. The capsules remain on the plant throughout the winter, and offer protection and shelter to overwintering ladybirds.

The leaves which grow from the root are oval, hairy and borne on long stalks. Those growing out from the stem are in contrast, paired, narrower and more lance-shaped, and grip the stem. They too are covered with soft hairs, as is the stem. The red campion grows to a height of between 1 and 2ft (0.3–0.6m). A perennial, it dies down in autumn, new leaves springing up early the following year.

The bright flowers have attracted the attention of many writers. 'The reddish-rose colour of its blossom makes it a very lovely ornament of the green hedge and affording one of the most pleasing contrasts imaginable,' said Margaret Plues in the nineteenth century. Especially where masses of the plants cover the hedgebank they are one of our most welcome wild flowers.

The Welsh name of *blodau'r neidr* means 'snake flower'. As well as soldier's buttons and bachelor's buttons, red campion—like many other plants with red flowers—has many local names which incorporate the word 'robin', such as robin's eye, robin-in-the-hedge and bob robin. An old superstition in many areas, still held by some older country people, suggested that death would come immediately to anyone foolish enough to pick the flowers.

STINGING NETTLE (*Urtica dioica*)
Most people know about stinging nettles, if only because of unhappy associations, particularly during youth! In fact there are two species, and it is ubiquitous perennial stinging nettle, not the annual species (*Urtica urens*), which is the one found commonly in hedgerows. As many gardeners know, once established it is difficult to eradicate— even small pieces of the underground rhizomes will send up stems. Of all the hedgerow herbs, the stinging nettle is probably the most widely distributed. Although it usually reaches no more than 3ft (1m) or so in height, on nitrogen-rich ground it manages to grow to 6 or 7ft (almost 2m).

The *dioica* in its name indicates that the male and female flowers occur on separate plants, though sometimes both may occur on one individual. Clumps of plants bearing the same-sexed flower will some-times grow together, simply because they have all arisen from the same underground rootstock. Both male and female blooms, which are on the plants any time from June to September, are small, pale green in colour, and hardly differentiated from the rest of the plant. But they have a complicated system for ensuring pollination: on a sunny day the filaments of a mature male flower will spring up, sending out puffs of pollen. These will land on the stigmas of female flowers close by. Although seeds are produced, most nettles spread via their underground rhizomes.

The plant's notoriety is of course due to its protective feature, the stinging hairs on the leaves and stem which release formic acid when touched; when they pierce the skin the acid enters and causes the pain.

Deaths from severe nettle stings have been mentioned by earlier writers, but nowadays this happens only in the rarest cases where someone has a violent allergic reaction to the poison.

The coarse, unattractive and now-despised nettle has had many uses in the past, especially as it is in leaf throughout much of the year. The Romans are supposed to have beaten parts of the body attacked by rheumatism with sprays of nettles.

In earlier times, before cotton was imported into Britain, nettles were cultivated and the fibres used for cloth-making. Fabric made from the plant was being woven in Scotland as late as the eighteenth century. Some nettle cloth from the late Bronze Age was discovered in a Danish grave, wrapped round the cremated remains.

The nettle is still used as a vegetable. Young, tender leaves taste akin to spinach, the formic acid being destroyed in cooking. In 1661, according to his diary, Samuel Pepys had a breakfast of nettle porridge, although how it was made, and what it tasted like, he never revealed. In *Rob Roy*, Scott the gardener actually grew a crop of nettles under glass, and these were used as 'early spring keil'.

In World War II chlorophyll extracted from nettles was used both for medicine and for camouflaging materials. Freshly made nettle tea was considered right for offering to guests in the mid-nineteenth century.

The nettle is also an important food plant for a whole range of invertebrate animals. The gorgeous peacock, small tortoiseshell, red admiral and comma butterflies all lay their eggs on it, so that their caterpillars can feed there once they have hatched. The first three are solely dependent on the stinging nettle; the comma lays on a number of different species, but most commonly on the nettle. Careful studies have shown that twenty-seven species of invertebrates are confined to the stinging nettle for food, with seventeen others feeding partly on it and partly on other herbs. Naturally these animals are themselves food for others, and so the nettle is vital to a whole chain of species. No part of the plant is safe from marauding invertebrates, which unlike large animals seem to be able to evade that sting! The sap in the stem and leaves is sucked by leaf hoppers and aphids, the leaves eaten by butterfly larvae and adult weevils, the flowers by small beetles, and when the fruits appear, they too will be the target for various bugs. Even the underground rhizome is not safe, weevil larvae extracting what nourishment they can from it. Yet unless vigorously tackled by over-tidy farmers or gardeners, the plant survives virtually undaunted.

VIOLET (*Viola odorata*)

As a truly wild species the sweet violet only occurs naturally in the south and east of England, where it grows under hedges and on sheltered banks. It has been planted in other parts of the British Isles, where it has become a naturalised species.

It is still one of the most loved and sought-after flowers of spring in areas lucky enough to have it. Growing early in the season, its small, delicately fragrant flowers brighten the lower realms of many hedge-rows.

Underneath the soil, it has a short rootstock, which sends out runners. The leaves, borne on long stems, grow out from the rootstock, heart-shaped in outline, the ends rounded or slightly pointed. Covered with a layer of fine hairs, they grow larger after the flowers have come and gone.

Some of the five-petalled flowers are blue, others white, with a variety of hues in between. As a general rule, the white-flowered species is to be found in the West and South-west of England and the purple variety in the Eastern and Midland counties. The petals, all of unequal size, form two pairs with one odd one, larger than the others, growing backwards in the form of a short hollow spur.

The sweet scent of the violet has never gone unnoticed, and two thousand years ago the flower was much sought-after for its perfume —probably first around the Mediterranean, but its fame spread and within a relatively short time it was valued throughout much of the European continent. The violet's perfume was linked with sex, and so this pleasant, hitherto almost insignificant species became known as a flower of Aphrodite, not to mention her son Priapus: indeed it soon acquired the Greek name of Priaperion.

Such tradition has been handed down through the centuries, and when the famous tapestry, the Hunt of the Unicorn, was designed, many historians assume for the wedding in 1519 of Francis I of France, and showed a number of flowers associated with sex in the final scene, the simple violet was included, vying with nobler species like blue-bells, lords-and-ladies and the early purple orchis.

The herbalists too took the violet, to make certain liquids which, reputedly, were 'bland, cool and soothing'. Among the medicants were 'syrup of violets' and 'oil of violet', made from a distillation of the petals.

Always noticed where it occurred in the countryside, like the primrose and the snowdrop, the violet attracted the usual superstitions. People in Gloucestershire were afraid to bring it indoors, for they held the strong belief that it would encourage fleas! In other parts of the country, violets inside were thought to have an adverse effect on the hens.

Along with the primrose, the sweet violet has decreased in numbers, as it has been uprooted from the hedgerows to be planted in gardens in town and country. The dog violet, of which there are several species, and which does not have the scent of the sweet violet, is now found flowering in many hedgerows in spring.

WOOD ANEMONE (*Anemone nemorosa*)
Although more typical of woodlands, the wood anemone occurs frequently along the shady side of hedgerows. Known by its alternative name of wind flower, from the Greek word *anemos*, 'wind', *nemorosa* indicates that it is a shade-loving species.

Like many of the early plants of the hedgerow the wood anemone is a perennial, the stems with folded leaves and rather drooping buds appearing in March or April, before many of the other hedgerow species have grown up.

Between half and two-thirds of the way up the stem are three leaves with deep clefts, fern-like in character, covered with soft, fine hairs. The other leaves grow nearer to the flower; larger and broader, they do not rise until the flowers have opened. White and delicate, sometimes with slight streaks of pink or purple on the undersurface of the six to eight petals, these flowers grow one to a stem. Although little pollen is produced there is an abundant supply of nectar, valuable food for any early-flying insects brave enough to face the cold March winds. In rain the flowers will droop, which protects the delicate inside. When pollinated the seeds develop in clusters which attract ants; they may carry the seeds for some distance from the parent plant.

Climbing Species

The hedgerow provides an extremely suitable habitat for many species of climbing plants. The big, showy white flowers of the greater bindweed (*Calystegia sepium*), which seems to flourish particularly well in warm summers, can often be seen until the first frosts in October, or as late as mid-November. Honeysuckle and the black and white bryony find plenty of support. Although these plants benefit from an occasional slice by the mechanical cutter or bill-hook, they appear to thrive better in less-managed hedges than in those which are continually trimmed and shaped.

BLACK BRYONY (*Tamus communis*)
Black bryony is totally unrelated to white bryony. Particularly common in the southern counties of England, it is widespread over much of the rest of the country excluding northern districts: where it is recorded for Scotland it is rare, and has been introduced, though it is found in Wales.

Black bryony is 'lost' in the impenetrable mass of other hedgerow plants for the greater part of the year. Unlike the white bryony it does not have tendrils, but its stem twines and winds its way around other hedgerow plants, turning in a clockwise direction as if following the sun. It will soon establish itself as a resident.

The leaves are larger than those of the white bryony, and are dark green in colour, heart-shaped and shiny. All leaves are turned towards the light. The very small light-green flowers arise in sprays from the point where the leaf joins the stem. It flowers from May until July. Flowers of one sex only occur on each plant, far more flowers being male than female.

John Clare, the Northamptonshire poet, was referring to black bryony when he wrote of 'scallop'd bryony' and indicated that its 'fine, bright leaves make up for want of flowers'. But however

IVY   TRAVELLER'S   HOP   BLACK
                                 JOY   BRYONY

inconspicuous the flowers, there are plenty of them, and once fertilized the female flowers form bright red berries which in autumn, as an earlier writer pointed out, 'festoon the hedges, frequently in gay abandon'. These strings of long-lasting berries add their colour to the ever-changing hedgerow ever more conspicuously as the leaves continue to fall from the bryony. When the berries first ripen they contain a substance distasteful to birds; this substance becomes modified later and birds will eventually eat them—though they are poisonous to us.

The underground stems, sometimes long and thick, will remain during the winter in the soil of the hedge bottom. It is from the colour of these that the plant gets the 'black' in its name. The stems contain an unpleasant poisonous substance which helps to protect them from attacks by hungry small mammals searching out food during the winter. Black as well as white bryony has acquired the 'mandrake' tag although the plants are not related.

Hedge bottoms provide a suitable habitat for the seeds to germinate, particularly where the hedges have not been actively managed.

BRAMBLE (*Rubus spp*)

Hedgerows abound with brambles, but no poet seems to have cared to celebrate the bramble. And yet how prolific it is, and what benefits it brings both man and other animals. In the British Isles, the name bramble or blackberry covers no fewer than four hundred identified micro-species.

A perennial plant, the thick, underground rootstock sends up innumerable thick stems covered with a number of defence 'mechanisms', including prickles and hooks and hairs which have glands at the tips, arranged in no particular pattern. The stems often grow to considerable lengths and arch over so that the tip touches the soil, where it will eventually root; in this way a new plant is formed and the bramble thicket spreads.

Like many hedgerow species the blackberry is a deciduous plant, its leaves falling in winter. In its first year, the compound leaves are composed of five leaflets. Second-year leaves have only three leaflets, serrated with a green, rough upper surface and a grey, slightly smoother underside. There are small hooked prickles on the underside of the leaf stem, and these continue along the midrib. During the third year of its existence, the stem dies away.

Because of the large number of different sub-species the flowers vary in colour and form, the petals being any shade from white to pale pink or mauve.

Where the blackberries have tip-rooted, large patches of the plant may have become established. From dawn to dusk in fine weather every spray of flowers will be swarming with life. Butterflies, such as small tortoiseshells, meadow browns and painted ladies, descend in hundreds to sip the sweet nectar. Bees and wasps, their wings beating almost incessantly and invisibly, swoop towards the flowers, land gently, their relatively heavy bodies sometimes causing the flower to sway momentarily, and quickly get to work. Brambles flower from June well into autumn, new flowers still appearing in October in some seasons, although these will not produce fruit.

The well-known succulent compound berry changes from green to pink, then red and finally glossy black and ripe, if the sweet-tasting fruits remain unpicked they too will attract a myriad of small creatures, including numerous species of insects, wasps in their thousands, and determined birds—and even the occasional fox or a hedgehog out for its last autumn fling before hibernation.

As so many common plants of the countryside, the bramble has a wide variety of local names, such as thief and country lawyer in Leicestershire. The fruits are called 'bumble kites' in Hampshire and Cumbria.

It is known that man has eaten blackberries for a long time. Their seeds were found in the stomach of a body, probably Neolithic, lying in clay close to the town of Walton-on-the-Naze, along the Essex coast.

To modern man the fruit is the only useful part of the bramble, but in the past it was of greater importance. The outer spine-covered skin of the stem was peeled away to leave a pliable rod, which country craftsmen used when thatching and for tying the twigs of besom brooms.

In some English churchyards a neatly plaited arrangement of blackberry stems was placed around the grave of a deceased person, either to keep the devil at bay, or to stop the body from leaving the grave. In a Cornish custom, seven bramble leaves were picked and purified in spring water, then placed on any inflamation or swelling; and the following was repeated three times for each of the seven leaves:

> There came three angels from the east.
> One brought fire and two brought frost.
> Out fire and in frost,
> In the name of the Father, Son and Holy Ghost.

In Scotland an orange dye was extracted from bramble roots. The leaves, again, were used for soothing swellings and burns. To keep evil spirits and witches away from houses, brambles, rowan and ivy were twined together.

CLEAVERS (*Galium aparine*)

A member of the bedstraw family, cleavers or goosegrass is unusual for a climber in being an annual; most are perennial. Although covered with minute hooks, it used to be much sought-after by geese, which ate its young green leaves: hence its alternative name.

Both stems and leaves have small, hooked bristles, and it is these which enable the floppy, straggling plant to attach itself to anything else in the hedgerow and so grow upwards; it can scramble for several feet in this way. Four to ten small leaves are arranged around the square stem.

In June and July the small, inconspicuous flowers appear, with their four white petals. These develop in autumn into the well-known small, round, hooked fruits. Green at first, they gradually darken with a purple tinge. Animals foraging in the hedgerow cannot brush past without collecting some of the seeds on their fur; humans gather them on their clothes. They cling with a vengeance and so are carried, perhaps over long distances, until they eventually drop off.

FIELD BINDWEED (*Convolvulus arvensis*)

To the gardener the field bindweed is a nuisance, a weed he can do without. Its creeping underground rooting system may cover as much as 332sq ft (30sq m) in one short season, and new plants will spring up from the tiniest fragment of root left in the soil.

In the hedgerow, however, its stems twine left to right, anticlockwise—unlike some other climbers—around any plants that will support it, including grasses and other species growing in and around the hedge bottom. It seldom manages to grow higher than a metre or so. A perennial, once entrenched in a hedgerow it usually spreads for a considerable distance.

The first flowers, their pink petals streaked and tinged with white, may appear late in May or early in June, and the bindweed usually blossoms well into September. The field bindweed reacts to being plucked, the exquisitely near-almond-scented flowers promptly closing their petals—as they do when it rains. Unlike the greater bindweed, this species also shuts its petals at nightfall.

GREATER BINDWEED (*Calystegia sepium*)

A rapid climber, greater bindweed adds its magnificent white bell-shaped flowers in profusion to the summer and autumn hedgerows.

In the competition for light in the often overcrowded hedgebank, the stems of this bindweed, like those of the smaller field bindweed, wind themselves around supporting plants anticlockwise; it may eventually reach a height of about 6ft (2m). The leaves are either egg-shaped or large, smooth, arrow-like and pointed, angled at the base.

White flowers generally stand out more clearly at night, and the greater bindweed is visited and pollinated by night-flying hawk-moths, their long tongues seeking out the nectar at the base of the flowers. More than two thousand years ago the Greek natural historian Pliny observed this.

HONEYSUCKLE (*Lonicera periclymenum*)

A tough, woody climber, the honeysuckle lacks tendrils or thorns, twines itself firmly around young trees, and does remarkably well. So tight is its grasp on a sapling that it may actually distort the growth of the tree, causing the trunk to twist like a corkscrew. Always turning in a clockwise direction, hedgerow honeysuckle may even climb the

BLACKBERRY

GREAT
BINDWEED

WHITE
BRYONY

CLEAVERS

trunk of a mature tree so that it can reach high enough above the other plants to receive plenty of the much-needed sunlight; it often outstrips the growth of a small tree. Once established it grows rapidly and may reach up to 20–25ft (say 6–7m). Not all plants find support; honeysuckle will also be found trailing around the ground.

The leaves unfold in April, growing opposite each other on the stem, elliptical—almost egg-shaped—in outline, their colour a dark green on the upper surface, more bluish on the underside, and with a slight sheen.

The flowers with their long, shaggy, petals will be in bloom from June to September. Most often cream-coloured, perhaps tinged with red or pink, some are white and there may be a whole variety of tints between. No two blossoms on a plant appear to be exactly the same colour. The sweet, heavy scent, particularly strong after dusk, attracts night-flying hawk moths which plunge their proboscis deep into the flowers' trumpets. As they extract the nectar, situated at the base of the corolla tube, they will also unwittingly deposit pollen from a previous flower. Petals may take on a deeper colour after pollination has taken place.

Pollinated female flowers produce clusters of deep red, round berries, which glow in the late summer and autumn hedgerow. If the surface of the berries has a rather tacky texture, they have been attacked by aphids which leave their mark with sticky honeydew. Standing out against the stark stems, the berries provide food for birds in autumn and winter. Country children used to nibble them, although they have little flavour.

Samuel Pepys, the great seventeenth-century diarist, was greatly taken by the flowers: the 'ivory bugles blow scent instead of sound', and not surprisingly this great lover of music dubbed the honeysuckle the 'trumpet flower'. Shakespeare in *Much Ado About Nothing*, commented that the honeysuckle 'ripened by the sun, forbids the sun to enter'. He had noticed how a successful plant that has twined its way upwards may have made so dense a growth below that the sun cannot penetrate its foliage.

Local names for the honeysuckle abound. In Somerset it is known as lamps of scent, suckles, gramophone horns; in Dorset as bugle bands;

in Devon as evening pride; in Yorkshire it is called bindweed and bindwood. In most counties the old name of woodbine is still known.

Writing in 1562 in his *Book of Simples*, William Britten sang the praises of the honeysuckle:

Ah how sweete and pleasant is woodbinde, in woods and arbours, after a tender, soft rayne, and how friendley doth this herbe, if I may name it, imbrace the bodies, armes and braunches of trees, wyth his long winding stalkes and tender leaves, opening or spreading forth his sweet lillies, like ladies fingers, emong the thornes or bushes.

IVY (*Hedera helix*)

A native plant, the evergreen, perennial ivy is commonly found interwoven amongst other hedgerow plants. A woody climber, it might at first appear to be parasitic on the tree, but this is not so. It is firmly rooted in the soil, competing for the available food materials there, probably quite close to the plant it uses for support. The trunk of an old tree heavily clothed with ivy has been mistakenly thought of as in itself an ivy tree!

Ivy may grow as a shrub or trail along the ground. The non-flowering shoots have the familiar five-lobed 'typical' leaves; the bushy flowering shoots have larger, less lobed leaves.

Shakespeare wrote in *A Midsummer Night's Dream* about the ivy which 'enrings the barky finger of the elm'; where it climbs up trees it may grow to a height of nearly 100ft (30m). To achieve its firm grip on trees or walls, its stems, which may measure up to 10in (25cm) in diameter, are liberally endowed with small adhesive roots.

Compared with most of the hedgerow species the ivy is late coming into flower, usually starting in September, although in some parts of the country not until October. The small clusters of yellow-green flowers have an unpleasant smell, although late insects, such as wasps and flies, are glad of the nectar, not on offer from many other species at this time of year. The flowers eventually form yellow berries, which ripen to a bluish-black colour in the following spring. These are useful food for several species of birds when other fruits are scarce.

Ivy: a useful food source for wildlife in late winter and early spring (*John Chard*)

TRAVELLER'S JOY (*Clematis vitalba*)
A lover of chalk and limestone soils, and found particularly in southern counties of Britain, the wild clematis, traveller's joy or old man's beard may grow to a height of 26–28ft (8m). Pushing itself upwards by means of twining leaf stalks, serving the same purpose as the white bryony's tendrils, it will then fall downwards, covering large areas of hedgebank with its flowers. Once it comes into contact with a shoot or stem it will hang on, establish itself, and thus scramble a long distance.

Several stems usually grow up from one single root, the leaf-stalk twining around any support available, including stems of their own species.

The compound leaves, the mid-veins of which have silky hairs, are made up of five yellow to green egg-shaped leaflets, which grow opposite each other on the stem.

Traveller's joy continues to bloom from July until September, the flowers growing in clusters at the end of short stalks. Having a slight, pleasant fragrance, and attracting many insects for their pollen, they have four small grey or greenish-white sepals turning outwards and downwards to reveal a yellow inside.

By autumn the familiar grey-feathered fruits sprawl over the hedgerow, giving the plant its other name of old man's beard. It was dubbed this by the herbalist John Gerard in the sixteenth century; he remarked that the plant was 'decking and adorning waies where people travell'.

WHITE BRYONY (*Bryonia dioica*)
White bryony is fairly common over much of the British Isles, but seems to thrive particularly well on chalky soils. Its tough, hairy, branching stem climbs by means of coiled tendrils which usually alter their direction half way along their length, supporting itself on the hedgerow bushes as it makes its way upwards to the sunlight. The green leaves have from five to seven lobes, the stalks arranged alternately on the stem, the centre one being longer than the others measuring up to 7in (17cm). They are not unlike vine leaves, but with much more distinctive pointed ends.

The greenish-white five-petalled flowers grow in clusters; male

Old man's beard—or traveller's joy or wild clematis—festoons the hedges in limestone country (*Goodman Photographics*)

flowers appear on one, females on another. Flowers are on the plant for several months, any time from about May through to August. Once pollinated the female flowers eventually develop into round, bright-red berries, and when the leaves have withered these add a bright splash of colour to autumn hedgerows. The berries are poisonous enough to kill a child rash enough to eat several.

Although the white bryony will die away during the autumn and winter, it is a perennial and the tuberous rootstock remains under the ground, starting to grow upwards when favourable conditions return in the spring.

The English white bryony acquired the intriguing reputation once preserved for the more illustrious mandrake: as an unrivalled aphrodisiac. Mandrake was extremely expensive to import, and the root of the white bryony apparently looked similar enough to work as a substitute—both for man and horses. If taken by a female unable to conceive, mandrake was believed to cause her to become pregnant.

The Bible quotes the instance of Rachel and Leah, and how the mandrake helped them (Genesis 30, verses 14–17). When the bryony roots were dug up, sometimes weighing as much as half a hundredweight (25kg), so the old herbalists inform us, their shape resembled the form of a child—or if it did not, then they were trimmed until it did! When ready they were hung in the old English herb shops, a tradition maintained even in the nineteenth century.

It was necessary to differentiate between the male and female varieties of the plant: it was the female variety which was given to stallion and man, and the male variety to mare and woman. As well as increasing fertility, it was thought to be a good general tonic for horses. Great care had to be taken to ensure that the correct dosage was used: if this was not carefully controlled, apparently the horse would get into an uncontrollable state.

8

The Everyday Hedgerow Birds

Of the larger animals which live in the hedgerow, birds undoubtedly make up the biggest group—in total numbers and in number of different species. When deciduous woodland covered the British Isles, this was naturally where the birds lived. As the woodland was gradually cleared by man, the birds had to change their habits to meet the new situation, and so they moved from compact areas of trees to clumps, and then to more isolated trees. Others went from thickets of dense vegetation to the narrow bands of it becoming available—the hedgerows.

The trees, once an almost universal and consistent feature of the hedgerow, have, in recent years, been vanishing, even if the rate of demolition is still uncertain. Deciduous woodland has, in the main, vanished from large parts of the British Isles. Yet most of the birds which once lived in this habitat are still classified as 'forest dwellers'. Although 7,000 years have elapsed since Neolithic man began to destroy our woodlands, so many of our commoner birds, like the warblers, tits, thrushes and blackbirds, have not adapted to live in a totally different environment; they still need some sort of thick cover if they are to survive. They need it for food, shelter and in many cases for a breeding habitat.

A few have adapted totally, including those like the lapwing and the skylark which have come to live with man's activities by nesting in the open fields he has made. But for most bird life, hedgerows are an important feature of the scene.

At the same time it should be remembered that even this habitat is relatively new. In those parts of the country which still have areas of deciduous woodland, the hedgerow is not as important as in barer places like East Anglia. Where hedgerows do occur in the vast open tracts of prairie-like country in Eastern England and parts of the Midlands, they are invaluable for birds; a life-giving oasis in a desert! Birds which formerly relied on woodland and latterly on hedgerows in these areas must be decreasing in numbers when extensive hedgerow removal takes place. If hedgerows are eventually eliminated altogether, as seems possible in some parts, then the birds which rely on them will inevitably go too; they will not be able to adapt to live in open areas.

Hedgerows are important in three ways for birds. As with animals

A flail-cut hedge. Ever more country hedges are being left in this splintered state; most seem to recover during a growing season. But for birds the cover for nesting is reduced (*Roy J. Westlake*)

The bird's enemy—mechanical hedge-cutting of some kind is near-universal along roadsides. At least the hedges are kept thick and solid (*Richard Mabey*)

in general, there are species which only come to the hedge to feed; other species feed and nest there; and yet others only need the hedge as a nesting site, taking their food from other habitats.

Those species which nest in the hedge can be grouped according to the zone they use. Hedges are of almost infinite variety, and so where one might support a vast bird population, another might not offer the right conditions and be almost devoid of life.

Starting at the bottom, we find the typical ground-nesting species, such as the pheasant, partridge and skylark, although the latter tends to move more into open fields. Moving up into the cover of low branches and shrubs, we find the robin, reed bunting and yellowhammer. Above, in the taller shrubs, are the greatest variety and number of birds. Those which use the hedge solely as a breeding place include the magpie and turtle dove. Those taking advantage of it both for breeding and feeding include the many common birds associated with farmland. Here song-thrush, long-tailed tit, sparrow and wood-pigeon will feed, build their nests and rear their young—and perhaps rear a cuckoo's young into the bargain.

Where hedgerow trees are found, trunks with holes will provide various species of owls with nesting sites. The wren, which often nests lower down in shrubs, will sometimes select a place up high. In the same area jackdaws, great tits, blue tits, starlings and tree sparrows will search for suitable sites. In areas where woodland trees are at a premium the greater spotted and green woodpeckers may make use of holes in hedgerow trees. High up in the branches of the tallest trees, the rook, wood pigeon, carrion crow and greenfinch will be found, sometimes joined by other species including mistle-thrush, tawny owl and buzzard.

Although many birds have managed to adapt to the hedgerow habitat, they have not always found it a totally satisfactory substitute for woodland. Indeed, such species as the nightingale and the majority of the tits will not breed in large numbers if adequate woodland can be found nearby.

Woodland margins are particularly important for wildlife, and support a varied fauna. Hedgerows, in some cases remnants of these woodland margins, are of course similar in ecological make-up. Whereas one acre of woodland may, for example, support two pairs of blackbirds, the same area of hedgerow may have anything up to four pairs. Aerial photographs show that hedges are valuable as 'pathways' linking larger areas, such as copse, spinney and woodland. Where these hedgerows are removed the link is broken and the larger areas probably become isolated. Animals inhabiting these large isolated areas may be able to begin to adapt to the conditions, but if they are unable to do so, then their numbers will drop and they could become extinct.

There are forty or so different birds in Britain which are termed 'farmland species'. Of these only a few, like the skylark, partridge and lapwing, could survive if there was no cover from either hedgerows or woodland.

It is difficult to make a comparision between areas, but the bird life of one of the few parishes in lowland Britain which has never been enclosed, Laxton in Nottinghamshire, has been studied. Here the Ministry of Agriculture, Fisheries & Food, the present owners, still practices a medieval system of cultivation, which has had interesting results. Because the area was never enclosed, the field boundaries lack trees, shrubs or hedges. The resident birds are confirmed as being those normally found where the old open-field system prevailed: lapwing, red-legged partridge, common partridge and skylark were the most characteristic species recorded.

A study has shown that during the early part of the year hedgerow birds spend their time either close to, or actually in, the hedge. Later, as crops ripen, the birds move into the fields where they find an abundant supply of food. The open-field species were found to be away from the hedge for much longer than other birds.

If a hedge is to support a valuable bird population it must meet a wide range of criteria, for example in density of cover, food sources, availability of song posts and of suitable trees. Although hedges in different areas will have a different mix of plants, which will influence the kinds and numbers of birds and animals using them, the method of management, or lack of it, is particularly important to the bird population. The 'best' type of hedge seems to be a very thick one which the farmer has allowed to grow up, but to which careful, rather than haphazard, management techniques are applied. Trees of different species and ages occurring along the length of a hedgerow will improve the variety of bird life.

Since 1962 the British Trust for Ornithology has been carrying out a Common Bird Census. The information for this is collected from various tracts of farmland throughout the British Isles. Because the survey is confined to this particular habitat, and excludes woodland, it is reasonable to assume that the birds covered are the commonest ones in our hedgerows. The large numbers of records collected show the most common birds as song thrush, yellowhammer, chaffinch, hedge sparrow, whitethroat, skylark, blackbird and robin. Of these species only one, the skylark, actually breeds in fields, the rest in hedgerows. Since it is a national survey, and averages have been taken, there are bound to be variations; in some areas, the linnet replaces one or other of the above species. Naturally there are changes in the list from time to time, but the general mix of species remains much the same.

BLACKBIRD (*Turdus merula*)
The blackbird has managed to adapt extraordinarily well to changing environmental conditions in the British Isles. In fact, along with one or two other species, including the chaffinch, it seems to have benefitted by man's expansion programme. Today it is one of the commonest species of resident breeding birds, probably second only to the chaffinch. Although it has taken to the hedgerows with some relish, it is also found in areas which man has more recently created: parks, gardens, squares and fields.

The blackbird belongs to the thrush family, the other two common breeding species being the mistle thrush and the song thrush. But the

BLACKBIRD

blackbird is the only one of the three with different plumage for the two sexes. Males and females are in fact very easily distinguishable. The hen bird, dark brown and slightly mottled, has a brown bill; the male, on the other hand, is genuinely black—his jet-black feathers highlighted by a bright yellow bill.

After finding suitable shrubs in the hedge, the younger, more inexperienced birds seem to build their nests first, sometimes before there are enough leaves to camouflage the structure. Dome-shaped, they are built by the female, using a mixture of dry grass and dead leaves mixed with mud. The first eggs usually appear in March and others will be found until July. The three to five eggs, a light blue-green broken up by brown spots, are incubated by the female for about thirteen days, and once the young have hatched she will be helped by her mate in the tiring round of feeding. Within a fortnight the chicks are fully fledged and ready to fly, although the parents still feed them after they have left the nest. Two or three broods are usual, but in a 'good' year there may be as many as five, and in a 'bad' year only one.

As its numbers have increased, the blackbird is now the mainstay of the dawn chorus, its strong, melodic song standing out amongst competitors. Many people consider that the blackbird's song is more tuneful than the nightingale's; certainly most of us are more likely to hear it.

There are two songs. One, sweet and muted, is sung through closed bill, and sounds somewhat like an echo in the distance. By far the more beautiful is the mellow fluting, so familiar throughout the country. The blackbird does have other calls: if danger threatens, even if a cat or bird of prey pass by without halting, it starts up an almost continuous and seemingly nervous chatter, trying raucously to scold and ward off the intruder. As dusk approaches, the bird utters the repetitive 'pink-pink' so much a part of the late evening countryside sounds.

CHAFFINCH (*Fringilla coelebs*)
If asked to name the commonest bird in Britain, most people would reply 'the house sparrow'. The bird, after all, is around, and takes advantage of, human beings and human habitations everywhere. But the bird which really tops the list is probably the chaffinch, closely followed by the blackbird.

A hedgerow species, the chaffinch was way ahead of the blackbird in numbers until the vast destruction of hedgerows in the last twenty years or so, when it lost large areas of its breeding habitat. Now, although it has not yet regained peak populations, it seems to be on the increase. Ornithologists still disagree, however, in spite of the Common Bird Census, and to be on the safe side often say that blackbird and chaffinch vie for the honour of being 'top hedgerow breeding species'! Certainly chaffinches are seen in built-up areas less frequently than either the robin or the blackbird.

They breed freely in hedgerows provided that the shrub species needed for nesting are available. They also want song posts from which to assert their territorial claims, so where there are trees they will usually be found in large numbers.

The male chaffinch has a handsome pink breast and cheeks, and a blue-grey head and neck. The back is chestnut, and there are white flashes on the shoulders, wings and tail. The female has yellow-brown plumage above, with a paler shading below. She has white feathers on the sides of the tail, as well as white wing-bars.

Both cock and hen assist with building a cup-like nest of moss and lichens, and the finished product is delightfully neat, the inside lined with a variety of materials, which may include hair, feathers and wool. Commonly found in amongst the shrubs which make up the hedge, the nest may also be in the trunk of a tree. Female chaffinches are ready to lay eggs from April through to early June. Off-white in colour, with red-brown blotches, the three to six eggs are incubated by the hen for thirteen to fourteen days. During the feeding of the young the birds change their normal habits, bringing caterpillars in particular, picked up from the leaves of trees. Adult insects are also caught, as well as earwigs and spiders. Two weeks after hatching and with a few false starts, the young will be on their way.

The song of the first birds will be heard in February, and ornithologists have discovered what appear to be dialects in different parts of the country. The variation of notes seems to be particularly evident in continental species which come to Britain in large numbers for the winter, seeking refuge from the colder climate of northern Europe. But in spite of these regional differences, it is not difficult to distinguish the bird's call, the end notes always being an emphatic 'Tissi-cheweeo'. Of its various calls the most common is undoubtedly 'pink, pink'.

Chaffinches need hedgerow trees in their living area, which will provide them with food. In general they will wait until food has fallen to the ground before they eat it, taking large quantities of small seeds, a multitude of which they find on arable weeds, common particularly along field margins and in and around hedgerows. Later in summer they scour cornfields for left-over grain, though the advent of the combine harvester has curtailed such supplies. Fields are often ploughed, or the stubble burned, almost before the corn has reached the drier, leaving few opportunities for the chaffinch.

Once breeding is finished for the year, chaffinches will join other members of the finch family, along with buntings and sparrows, to make up large flocks which swoop, dive, twist and turn across arable fields and over hedgerows, in their eager search for food to satisfy a seemingly ever-present hunger. Disturbed whilst feeding in a field, a vast flock may rise and fall in an almost rhythmical troop. Although flocks of chaffinches usually include both males and females, occasionally they consist entirely of one sex.

GREENFINCH (*Carduelis chloris*)
The upper branches of hedgerow trees provide a nesting site for the greenfinch, and it will feed in the hedge as well. Typically found in open countryside, the bird still needs bushes, trees and hedges for shelter and food. Olive-green in colour, it has yellow streaks on the sides of the tail and yellow wing-bars. The hen bird is less brightly marked than the cock.

The greenfinch has become an opportunist, taking advantage of man's impact on the countryside. Nowadays it is found in parks and gardens, where shrubberies and food on bird tables supplement the diet collected from the hedgerows. Greenfinches often move around in mixed flocks which include linnets, chaffinches, yellowhammers and tree sparrows. Together they search the weedy wastes and stubble fields looking for food in autumn and winter. Although most of the greenfinches in these mixed flocks are home-bred, their numbers are augmented by migratory birds. Feeding peacefully, a sudden noise causes them to panic. They rise up quickly with an almost rebounding flight movement, accompanied by a whirring of wings, the intensity of sound depending on the number in the flock. At the same time they utter a displeased, wheezy, twittering sound. Under these conditions most greenfinches will leave the mixed flock and form one of their own kind, often flying for a considerable distance, returning when they think the coast is clear. But the flight path they take is far from straight; they circle and swoop, no bird following exactly the line of the one in front. Eventually they come back to their original feeding place. Their suspicions are still not allayed, and before coming down to look for food they circle and swoop again in an all-out effort to check and double-check that the disturbance has now passed and the place is safe. Convinced at last, they land silently and continue feeding as if nothing had disturbed them.

The bird's usual call is a monotonous wheezy nasal 'tsweee', but it has a fine song-flight display often overlooked. It flies up to a suitable height and then fully extends both tail and wings; the yellow markings, usually seen only in short flashes, are revealed to the full for all to see. Once in this position the flight of the bird is slow and unsteady, and covering a wide circle it will eventually land on the perch it probably left but a few moments before. When performing on the wing, its song is much sweeter. It always starts with its typical wheezing notes, but these culminate in a series of longer notes which have been compared in quality to those of a woodlark.

This performance is not seen very often, even in areas with a lot of greenfinches. It may be a desperate effort on the part of the cock to advertise his presence in the hope of attracting a still-unattached hen. Such displays usually work, apparently because later investigations have shown nests in the area, when there had been none before.

The cup-like nest is an untidy affair, consisting of moss, roots and grass, the interior lined with roots. The first eggs are laid late in April and it is not unusual to find a female sitting on a clutch in August. Four to six eggs vary in shade from white to pale blue, the surface broken with reddish-brown streaks and spots. Greenfinches are seed-eaters, but they will for a time collect animal material for their off-spring, soon putting them on to a solely vegetarian diet.

Within a fortnight the fledglings are ready to fly. Although the adult birds usually stay in the same area, where they will probably rear a second brood and even perhaps a third—young in the nest can be discovered in late August and early September—the newly fledged birds will quickly disperse, often travelling considerable distances from the nest. Some birds will even make their way to the continent.

The shape of the stout bill is such that the bird can eat food of varying sizes. Greenfinches will actually raid fields of corn in late summer, pulling the seed from the still-standing stems; come the winter months, they will seek the hips of the wild rose, stripping away the flesh to get at the seeds inside. In spring and summer they feed on the seeds of many common weed species.

HEDGE SPARROW (*Prunella modularis*)

The hedge sparrow, or dunnock, seems an integral, if inconspicuous, part of hedgerow life. Although the bird is similar in size and markings to the house sparrow, its bill is more slender and not so blunt. The head has a grey eye-stripe, and there is grey on both the throat and breast. The brown back feathers are broken with darker streaks. Both cock and hen birds have similar markings.

A true hedge species in every way, as its name implies, the hedge sparrow both builds its nest and feeds there. But unlike the house sparrow, commonly seen for most of the day, the hedge species is more secretive, skulking in the hedge for much of the daytime, emerging occasionally to feed. It gives away its presence by its high piping call, heard for much of the year although there is usually a period of silence towards the end of summer. The bird is probably timid and prefers to live a solitary existence.

Although it is now a hedge-dwelling species, the dunnock has been in Britain since long before hedges were commonplace. In earlier days people did not really study the birds around them, and a number of species about the same size as the dunnock were dubbed 'sparrow'. Many have been sorted out and renamed, but the hedge sparrow has been stuck with the name. Known in medieval times as 'sugge', there are still places with 'sug' in their names: amongst these are Sugham in Surrey and Sugworthy in Devon, and possibly Sugnall in Shropshire.

DUNNOCK

The bird's alternative name, dunnock, is a country word meaning 'dun-coloured'.

The dunnock's thin bill in fact is enough to show that it is primarily an insect-eater, not a seed-eater like the house and tree sparrows with their thick beaks. In autumn when insects and their larvae become scarce, the dunnock turns its attention to spiders and earthworms. In winter it must again change its eating habits, living almost entirely on small seeds. Most food is taken on the ground, the bird moving forward with a hopping movement.

At one time, according to John Ray writing in 1678, ladies would wear the delicate-coloured eggs of the hedge sparrow as ornaments—after, of course, they had been blown!

Because it is one of the most common hedgerow species, the hedge sparrow's nest and eggs frequently merit the attention of the parasitic cuckoo: some naturalists think it suffers more than any other hedgerow bird, particularly in southern counties. Gilbert White wondered why the hedge sparrow is fooled into incubating the eggs of the cuckoo, which are so much larger and so different in colour: the hedge sparrow could not have much idea of the difference between its own eggs and the replacements foisted upon it. The cuckoo frequently uses the nests of meadow pipits, but here its eggs bear similar markings to the host's—an evolutionary development to ensure that the eggs are accepted.

Hedge sparrows prefer hedgerows with thick cover close to the ground or where the hedgebank has a dense covering of nettles and brambles. They build a bulky cup nest of moss and grass, lined with mixed wool and hair. The hen lays between three and five eggs, of a delicate pale blue, and sits on them for nearly two weeks. Once the young emerge, the cock bird will assist his mate with pushing endless supplies of food into open mouths, but twelve days or so after hatching, flight comes easily to the young dunnocks, and they are ready for independence.

The first eggs are usually laid in late March, and once that brood is flying a further batch of eggs will usually be laid and incubated. Sometimes three broods are recorded, the last eggs being laid in early July.

LINNET (*Acanthis cannabina*)

The linnet, with its chestnut back, white bars to its wings and white sides to its tail, was once the delight of ladies, particularly in Victorian and Edwardian times. The male's summer plumage—a fine crimson crown and breast—was much admired. Having a pleasant, if twittering song which it performs with alacrity and perhaps even a touch of eccentricity, the linnet was shamefully often kept as a caged pet. Fortunately the craze for this has long passed.

The bird has the distinction of being the commonest member of the family of small finches; its relatives include the redpoll and the goldfinch. Its flight, like that of other small finches, is, to put it mildly, what the bird books call 'erratic'. A linnet never seems to fly from one spot to another in a straight line; it follows a zigzag path even for a short distance. All of this is carried out with a distinct flair and flourish, as if to proclaim that even a simple act like flying from A to B can be a pleasant pastime.

Particularly gregarious by nature, especially during food-seeking excursions, linnets also seem to sing in chorus. The movements of flocks, as of single birds, is erratic and uninhibited, and all birds seem to follow the same ups and downs although the actual line of flight is

LINNET

individualised. Their apparent love of companionship is again shown by their tendency to nest in groups or colonies in a given area.

Hedgerows carry the nests of many thousands of linnets every year. As they are often built before the hedge is clothed with leaves, they can be particularly conspicuous. Bushes, and in particular gorse bushes where they grow, are chosen for nest sites, and the female will start the building, using grass and moss for the main part of the nest and gathering wood and hair for the lining. The linnets may lay their first four to six eggs in April, but because there are two and possibly three broods, eggs may be found as late as July. Light blue in colour, the shells are marked with a few red-purple blotches. Incubation, for eleven days, is mainly the concern of the hen, although the cock bird may help out from time to time. He is more concerned about the nestlings once they have hatched. After twelve days the birds are ready to leave the comfort and relative safety of the nest, making way for the next family.

Seeds of many common weeds are taken for food, though nestlings are fed some insects, mainly caterpillars. Where a cuckoo has been foolish enough to lay an egg in a linnet's nest it seems unlikely that its young will survive, once hatched. The linnet's specialised diet is mainly made up of weed seeds which the young cuckoo is unable to take, and it will starve in the nest.

Choosing a suitable song post, perhaps on a fence stake or hedgerow bush, the linnet will sing its heart out, particularly in an effort to gain a mate. In flight it utters a twittering sound, something like 'zee-chee-chee'; when alarmed this changes to 'tsoo-eet'. Ready for the courtship fray, and desperate for a mate, the cock bird lets forth a series of sweet-sounding notes and at the same time spreads and hangs down its tail with a rapid, urgent, almost nervous shaking of the feathers: all of which, hopefully, will ensure that a hen is attracted.

PARTRIDGE (*Perdix perdix*)

The partridge is a solid-looking game bird but much smaller than the pheasant, and much drabber in appearance—even the cock. The overall brown plumage is broken by bars of chestnut on the flanks; the tail is also chestnut. The underparts of the neck are white, and there is a brown horseshoe-like shape on the breast.

In some places the bird is known as the Hungarian partridge, a name derived from the fact that large numbers of birds were imported from Europe, especially from Hungary. Most partridges, like pheasants, were bred specifically for sport, although these are generally 'wild' birds. The first of September is the beginning of the shooting season, and at this time partridges are living in family groups or coveys. The start of the breeding season, towards the end of January or the beginning of February, is marked by the break-up of these groups. The cock birds start to assert their supremacy, vigorously defending their territory, displaying aggressively to retain control of their own patch. Courtship varies: sometimes exuberant birds will take to the air in their breeding pairs, flying after each other in what seems to be a game of 'catch me if you can'.

Hedgerow vegetation provides the hen bird with plenty of cover for her nest. Simply making a scrape in the ground, she then adds a comfortable lining of dried grass and leaves. A distinct pathway often leads from the nest into the field, the bird's regular route when obtaining food. After mating she will lay a large clutch of pale olive eggs, twelve to eighteen of them, towards the end of April or early in May. The twenty-four-day period of incubation is the hen's concern, but the partridge cock, unlike the pheasant, will look after the chicks once they have hatched. They leave the nest within a few hours, waiting only for their wet feathers to dry. Within two weeks they will be taking their first tentative flight lesson.

The hedge, the field and its margin provide the partridge with a wide variety of food, which includes flowers, leaves, buds, grain and seeds taken from short vegetation. Animal food also forms an important part of the diet—snails, slugs and a variety of insects, as well as spiders.

PHEASANT (*Phasianus colchicus*)
The hen pheasant, like the partridge, often nests beneath the thick vegetation of a hedge bottom. Here she makes a scrape in the ground, lining it with a few grass stems and leaves. Occasionally she may use the discarded nest of some other bird in a tree. Eight to fifteen eggs, pale olive in colour, will be laid late in April or early in June. Incubation lasts twenty-two to twenty-seven days, the hen coping alone with this and with rearing the chicks. As is common with ground-nesting birds, the young leave the nest a few hours after hatching and within twelve to fourteen days are capable of flying.

The pheasant was brought to Britain many centuries ago, and it has been claimed that the Romans introduced it, though there is no real evidence one way or the other. The first definite record of the bird as a British breeding species comes from 1059, just before the Norman Conquest. A native of Asia, the pheasant species brought to Britain came from the Caucasus, but later in the eighteenth century other species were introduced; one had a white neck-ring, and inter-breeding has resulted in about half our present pheasant population having the neckband and half being without.

The pheasant's feathers are mainly copper in colour, those of the hen being slightly darker and more brownish. She is much drabber than the cock, who is a conspicuously handsome bird, with an iridescent purple-green sheen on the head, red wattles around the eyes, and magnificent long tail feathers. The male is around 32in (82cm) long, of which 18in (45cm) is accounted for by the tail. The female, at 22in (57cm), has a tail of 9in (22cm), half the length of the male's.

The pheasant will find plenty of food in a thick, mixed hedgerow, since its diet is very varied. Fruits, seeds and leaves of wild plants are complemented with a wide variety of insects, including wireworms, leatherjackets, grasshoppers and caterpillars. Where food is scarce, pheasants may take small species of birds, as well as voles and lizards.

REDWING (*Turdus iliacus*)
Coming from Northern Europe, where the climate is much harsher than in the British Isles, the first redwings usually arrive here in September, staying until April when the worst of the cold has gone. Although still very much a migrant, the redwing has been breeding regularly in Scotland since 1953. The first nest was discovered in Sutherland in 1925, and in the ensuing twenty-eight years the bird bred in Scotland from time to time. It now seems to have established a breeding colony.

Related to the mistle thrush, fieldfare and blackbird, the redwing is the smallest member of this family in Great Britain. Redwings and fieldfares are often seen together feeding during their winter stay. Even in this country they still die in large numbers when the weather is so severe that they are unable to dig into the frozen soil in search of earthworms. They scour the countryside for hips and haws and other wild fruits, so are frequent visitors to our winter hedgerows.

The redwing is slightly smaller in size than the song thrush which it resembles. The tell-tale differences are the patches of red feathers under the wing and on the flanks. A further identifying feature is the very conspicuous white stripe over the eyes.

If the bird nests in Britain, the cup is set on a layer of twigs and soil and often decorated with mosses and lichen. In Scotland it has a preference for birchwood, but in the hedgerow it may use a bush or tree, or simply make its home on the ground. The female alone is probably responsible for nest-building.

The eggs are likely to be laid from May to July, four to six in the

REDWING

clutch and of a blue-green colour, the surface broken with red-brown marks. Whether both parents help with incubation is uncertain. The nestlings emerge after thirteen days and both parents bring food. In fourteen days or so the young are ready to fly.

British redwings seldom utter their true song. The note heard most often is a high-pitched 'see-ih', frequently repeated by the birds as they fly overhead at night.

ROBIN (*Erithacus rubecula*)
Robins, familiar to all of us as they are lovers of human company, particularly during unfavourable feeding conditions in winter, are another woodland species that has taken to the hedgerow in search of new nesting sites. Provided that there is a thick layer of undergrowth, they can be comfortably accommodated there.

The robin, with its olive-brown back and flanks, highlighted by the

145

famous orange-red breast, the colour of which also extends over the throat and onto the forehead, is known to everyone from childhood. Cock and hen birds look similar.

As one of Britain's most popular birds, particularly in the country, it was not surprising that the robin was chosen as Britain's national bird—though not without much soul-searching. In 1961 the British Section of the International Council for Bird Preservation was asked to nominate a national bird, and this did not prove too easy—and caused a protracted correspondence in *The Times*! Few are likely to argue with the choice. David Lack, whose book *The Life of the Robin* is a bird-study classic, reckoned that the bird almost shows 'affection' for man and has come to live where man lives because of the British character. On the continent, where it is probably as common, it is seldom seen around human habitations, and the Europeans consider it a shy bird. In Britain it will perch close to the gardener, ever-watchful for the tasty worms his digging and tidying may reveal, its eager eye spotting the slightest movement on soil or path.

Although it appears so good-humoured and almost tame, this behaviour belies the robin's true character, particularly during the mating season. Robins, like many other birds, have territories. To a robin its territory is its home, almost its fortress, to be defended vigorously, and if need be violently, against would-be intruders. Its melancholy song is repeated almost incessantly as a means of letting fellow robins know the extent of its patch. It pauses at intervals, during which other robins sing out their plaintive cry, and the whole pattern of robin territory within an area can reveal itself to a careful listener.

The hen robin has her own territory, too, which she patrols during the winter, though too busy with nesting and feeding young in summer. Her boundaries are marked by her own frequently warbled song. Throughout the year, with a slight lapse in July when it moults, the robin keeps up its territorial claims. Only in very severe weather, when the overriding instinct must be to survive and the robin is out desperately searching for food, does the urge to defend its territory take second place; only then will it allow an intruder to cross the boundaries of its patch.

The female builds a domed nest with grasses, dead leaves and moss,

ROBIN

and the eggs may be laid any time from March through to June,
usually three to six in a clutch. Their white ground colour is marked
with a variety of reddish-brown spots and blotches. The hen incubates
the eggs for about two weeks, and when the chicks have pushed their
way through the protective shell the cock plays his part in their up-
bringing. After about two weeks the young can fly, and the adults turn
their attention to another brood.

With new birds in adult plumage appearing in late summer, the
established territories have to be closely guarded. Life is difficult for all
concerned until eventually each bird has decided on its territorial limits.

The middle of winter may not be the best time to choose a mate, but
cock robins sing heartily from suitable trees to attract the hens, a
familiar winter sound. Once a hen has intimated that she may be
willing, she is suffered to enter the cock's territory, where she stays
for several weeks. Should he decide that she appears to be an acceptable
mate, she is allowed to stay and will then actively join him.

ROOK (*Corvus frugilegus*)
Where there are numbers of tall trees in or near hedgerows, a colony
of rooks will usually take advantage of them. Rooks are often confused
with carrion crows: from a distance they do look similar in colour,
build and length. In overall shading the rook is black, the feathers
having a purple gloss. On the face there are bare grey-white patches
which also occur at the base of the bill. The thick feathers around the
thighs give the bird what some naturalists call a 'baggy breeches' look.
The sexes look alike.

The age-old phrase 'as the crow flies' should really be 'as the rook
flies', for it is the latter that makes daily excursions to and from its
home, the tree-top rookery. Both Shakespeare and Tennyson seem to
have considered crows and rooks as the same species—Tennyson's
'many-wintered crow that leads the clanging rookery home' is as misleading as Shakespeare's 'light thickens and crows make wing to the
rooky wood!'

The rook bears no resemblance to the crow when it comes to lifestyle. Rooks live a noisy, sociable, communal existence. They go off
in search of food in flocks, nest and live in a close-knit community, but
nevertheless they do have strong territorial rights. A pair of rooks will
aggressively defend an area around their nest against all comers. The
idea of rooks holding 'parliaments' has probably arisen from this, for a
bird attempting to enter the territory of others will be surrounded by
the rightful inhabitants: the intruder looks as if seated at the centre of
proceedings.

During the courtship period the male offers food to the female (an
activity which he repeats when she is sitting on the eggs). Part of his
display in wooing his mate includes an almost incessant cawing and
bawling. Once the rooks have selected a nesting site, high in the trees,
the area will be used for many years. When the leaves have fallen from
the trees in the autumn the colony of untidy nests, probably made
worse by the activities of the nestlings, is all too evident.

A tree selected, both cock and hen birds set to nest building, piling
up sticks for the framework and lining the interior with a combination
of leaves, roots and dried grass. The untidy heap remains the birds'
permanent property: next year they will repair any damage, adding

ROOK

more sticks and enlarging the nest, which does nothing to enhance its appearance. The nest completed or repaired, the hen is ready to lay in late March or early April. Three to six pale green to grey or even blue eggs are laid, their surface marked with grey and brown streaks and blotches. The female sits on the eggs for about eighteen days, the cock attending her with food. The young out, both parents share in the feeding, which lasts for about a month, after which the fledglings are ready to leave.

If the spring rookeries are impressive, the winter roosting sites, where hordes of birds assemble, are spectacular and known for miles around. A central rookery warrants the attention of all rooks living within 5 or 6 miles (9km). To reach it they behave much as starlings do when coming back to their roost. Groups of birds, some large, some small, others straggling, make their way towards the trees. But they do not enter immediately; instead they alight in tall trees some distance from their ultimate destination. Here they wait, noisily and in what must appear to the onlooker to be a state of great agitation, for the rest of the birds to arrive. By the time that all have gathered, the trees may be bearing the weight of perhaps 5,000 or 6,000 birds, accompanied by perhaps as many as 2,000 jackdaws. The cawing reaches a crescendo— and then, as if at the signal of an unseen leader, it stops. In silence the birds leave the tree tops. Swooping silently, except for the sound of their beating wings, they land on the ground. Here they seem to be searching for food before, quite unexpectedly, they rise and make their way to their final roosting site to spend the night. The hush has been broken again, the loud, almost yapping voices accompanied by the swish of 5,000 pairs of wings in what sounds like some vast choir and orchestra, with here and there a soloist breaking through. Ultimately the noisy birds will calm down.

Autumn, too, sees well-timed aerial displays: high above the trees the birds twist, tumble, and then plummet headlong towards the ground below.

To some farmers and country people the rook is a 'friend'; to others a definite 'foe', for its taking of crops, its noise and untidiness. Rooks eat grain, but at harvest time although the quantity may be large, most of it is scavenged from the ground; in addition, they do take pests— wireworms and leatherjackets in particular are much relished—and they also eat snails, earthworms and various insects and their larvae. They will eat fruit, seeds and grain, and sometimes carrion.

SONG THRUSH (*Turdus philomelos*)
Whereas its relative the blackbird has increased in numbers, probably having a population explosion as it has invaded new habitats, the song thrush's fate has been the opposite—even though it too has learned to live in gardens. Over the last ten to twenty years, its numbers have been decreasing steadily. Blackbirds occupying hedgerow sites far outnumber the thrushes.

Yet since 1962 the Common Bird Census has shown that the song thrush is still one of the ten commonest hedgerow-breeding birds. Both cock and hen have a mottled plumage of brown above, paler under-parts, golden-buff underwing and spotted buff breast. Smaller in size than the mistle thrush, the song thrush lacks the latter's characteristic white on the tail feathers.

Watching a song thrush hopping across the lawn or moving about the foot of the hedge, you will see it pause at frequent intervals and cock its head to one side; it is easy to assume it is trying to hear the worms or insects moving below the turf or in the leaves. A glance at the bird will correct you—the eyes are at the side of its head, so it tilts its head to see the ground. Rather than listening for food the bird is—of course—looking for it!

Both cock and hen birds build the nest; in a hedgerow it may be placed in a bush, shrub, or low tree. It is as well that they both pitch in, because they like a bulky cup-shaped nest, made from dead leaves and dry grass, the interior lined with mud. The three to six light blue, black-spotted eggs are laid there between March and July, and incubated for about a fortnight by the female. Both parents share the search for food, bringing a selection of insects and their larvae, as well as snails

SONG THRUSH

and earthworms to the hungry nestlings. Two weeks, and many, many worms, after hatching, they will be ready to fly. The first brood successfully reared, there may be two more in a season.

Robert Browning, ever-mindful of his love of England and things English, was aware of the distinction between the call of the song thrush and that of the mistle thrush and the blackbird. 'Home Thoughts from Abroad' expressed it:

> That's the wise thrush; he sings each song twice over
> Lest you should think he never could recapture
> The first fine careless rapture

Of course Browning was right, but sometimes each phrase, distinctly made and clearly audible, may be repeated more than twice. While the bird's song is particularly noticeable in the warmer days of spring, the clear, melodiously phrased song starts as early as January in fair weather and there will be hardly a break from its notes until July. Then the thrush seems to rest for a couple of months or so. Come September it starts to sing again, and on any fine, bright days in October and November it can be heard as clearly and loudly as it was way back in early spring.

A thrush's anvil is something you will often find in the countryside. Having located a good supply of snails, the thrush will search out a suitable stone on which to crack open their shells with a few sharp, swift blows, and round a favourite stone will be a large scattering of broken shell. Earthworms are also an important part of the bird's diet. To these can be added insects and their larvae, as well as a variety of berries, fruits and seeds.

WHITETHROAT (*Sylvia communis*)
In areas where overgrown hedges are found, the whitethroat—a warbler—is a likely breeder. Spending the winter in Africa, it arrives in Britain in April, announcing itself with its song, rather short and sweet, from the top of the tallest bush around. Once here it will spread far and wide over the British Isles where conditions are suitable.

Some birds are very particular about their choice of mates, but the

WHITETHROAT

male whitethroat seems less fussy. Sometimes he will actually woo and win the first hen brave enough to enter his territory. The courtship ritual is often rough, and not just on one side. The cock bird, taking to the wing with a strand of grass in his bill, flies closely behind the hen. Almost unexpectedly and seemingly without provocation, he will suddenly dash at her, at the same time serenading her with song. Not pleased, or playing not pleased, with such an unwarranted attack, the female takes the law into her own hands: with outstretched wings and tail she makes a sudden springing movement, in an effort to send the male off. As if playing a game of 'chicken', he stands in her path until the last moment, jumping aside to avoid the actual attack.

Nest-building seems to be even more laborious than for most other birds. The male sets about building a series of nests, sometimes finishing three or more. The female is usually unimpressed with the male's efforts. If she cannot bring herself to settle for any of them, both birds will set about the building operation together. A selection of grasses is brought to the chosen site, often close to the ground in dense cover, and a cup-shaped nest is completed, lined with horse hair and some-times decorated with down. Four or five eggs may be laid from about May until July, green or pale buff in base colour, with grey markings. The nestlings, attended by both parents, are fully fledged at eleven days, and there are generally two broods.

WREN (*Troglodytes troglodytes*)
After the goldcrest, the wren is our smallest bird, and has for a long time been looked on with affection. Perhaps it is its busy, cheeky, attitude which endears it to us as it stands with its little cocked-up tail, uttering its trilling, piercing song, or scuttles in and out of the ivy leaves. Its red-brown coat, barred on the tail, flanks and wings, its small size and that absurd tail, make it an unmistakable everyday bird throughout Britain.

Where ivy-covered trees are found in the hedgerows, the wren chooses to hide its nest in the creeper. The cock wren in fact builds several nests, domed structures made from a mixture of leaves, moss and grass. His next important job is to encourage a hen bird to choose one of them. When she has done so, she puts her own finishing touches to it by lining it with feathers, taken in through the side entrance.

The first eggs are laid from the end of April onwards. White in colour, they have delicate red-brown spots. Within the usual fortnight, after almost continuous incubation by the hen bird, they hatch, and after fifteen days the young are ready to fly. The male may continue to be protective, and escort the newly flown birds to one of the nests which the female had previously rejected. Here he will tend them for a time, while the female gets on with the task of laying and incubating a second brood.

Whether the wren has a mate in every nest seems to be dependent on the food supply. With a good source of small insects and larvae, he may support hens in several of these 'homes' he put together so laboriously earlier in the season. If food is not plentiful, then he will make do with one hen.

Although wrens are quite common all over Britain they do suffer drastic reductions in population after prolonged severe weather in winter. Because of its small size, the bird loses a higher proportion of its heat, via its body surface, than larger birds. After the very severe spell of weather, lasting for many weeks, in the winter of 1962–63, on average only one third of the wren population is thought to have survived; in some places much less than this. However, provided that there is a small nucleus of birds left to carry on breeding, the numbers soon recover. It seems that more young survive in the following years in compensation.

The wren does do something to help itself in cold weather. Whereas it usually spends the night roosting in bushes in the open, in a severe spell it seeks out its own nest, or will make use of a deserted house martin's nest or even a man-made nest box. When the cold becomes intense, it goes even further: several birds will huddle close together, each helping to conserve the others' warmth. Ten wrens have been found huddled inside the shell of a coconut!

YELLOWHAMMER (*Emberiza citrinella*)

Flitting from hedge to hedge across a narrow country lane is where yellowhammers will typically be found: in the countryside, away from habitations. Generally (though not always) they shun areas of human settlements. Yet the bird does not really seem to have any aversion for people; indeed sometimes it seems to be us whom it is serenading from a suitable bough along some quiet stretch of hedgerow. Its familiar call, usually translated as 'little-bit-of-bread-and-no-cheese', or in Scotland as 'deil-deil-deil-deil-tak'-ye', is familiar to most country people.

It is the cock which seeks out a hedgerow bush to utter those six repetitive, almost staccato, notes terminated by a prolonged near-wheeze. The hedgerow is its stage; here it will perform to anyone or no one, caring not whether it has an audience. Starting towards the end of February its distinctive call echoes round the country lanes until about August, and it may continue singing until the first weeks of November. Though most frequently seen around hedgerows, where numbers are quite high in some places, it will also take to more barren, open heaths or commons, even where boundaries are but dykes. Here too it will sing, provided of course that it can find a suitable song post. It is resident over most of the British Isles, though rare in the Hebrides.

The cock bird woos a possible mate, late in March or early in April, with his courtship display. She, seemingly playing 'hard to get', takes to the wing in twisting and erratic flight; he is not to be beaten and follows her closely. At last he catches up with her, and both birds fall to the ground together, where mating generally follows. Sometimes a cock bird will parade before the hen, circling her in a fine assertion of superiority over others, holding his head-crest erect and spreading out his wings and tail. Rarely can a hen bird reject such a fine show of male supremacy, and she eventually accepts the cock as her mate.

The commonest of the buntings in Britain, yellowhammers are seed-eating birds, with stout, pointed bills. The cock has the distinction of being able to exhibit a greater area of yellow feathers than any other British bird except the yellow wagtail. The bright yellow head and breast are subtly marked with darker chestnut streaks, which are highlighted against the much darker brown of the back and wings. Although the female is still classified as a 'distinctive yellow bird' her colours are softer than the male's, and she has more brown streaks, with a chestnut rump and white feathers along the sides of the tail.

The hen bird is responsible for building the nest, which may be close to or even on the ground, in among ivy or perhaps on a bank or wall. Using dried grasses for the basic structure, she will line the inside with softer, finer grasses and hair. The spot chosen will be secluded, and once built the nest is well hidden. Two to five white or pale pink eggs, marked irregularly with purple-brown or brown, are laid any time from April to August. The female sits on them for about thirteen days, and both parents help with feeding the young. Although buntings are seed-eaters for the greater part of the year, the young are fed on an insect diet, large numbers of caterpillars being needed. After twelve days they are taking flight lessons, and the parents are preparing a second egg-laying session—and a third in some seasons.

Once mating and the rearing of young have finished, yellowhammers come together and large flocks are often to be seen raiding stubble fields, searching for any grain left when the harvest was gathered, though little remains with today's harvesting methods. The British birds may be joined by migrating flocks from Europe, although the home-bred birds seem to spend their lives in one area.

9

Mammals

With few exceptions, birds are easily seen in the hedgerows, but for mammals quiet observation is needed. Certain species are found in hedgerows—amongst other habitats—almost universally throughout Britain.

Hedgehogs often live at the hedge bottom, and even when resident will move out to other areas in search of food. Some animals now look to the hedgerow for protection, and this is probably true of the mole. It used to live most often in—or under—open fields, but has sought refuge in the hedge as more and more arable land becomes intensively cultivated. From its sanctuary the mole can move back and forth into the field on its almost incessant tunnelling and food-hunting expeditions.

A smaller animal consistently found in hedgerows, and often responsible for a labyrinth of underground tunnels, is the bank vole. Its nest is sited above or below ground according to the amount of cover available.

Of several species of mice known to live in hedges, by far the commonest is the long-tailed field mouse. It lives underground, digging itself two chambers, one for storing food, and the other for sleeping. Long-tailed field mice often have communal nests, collecting together a store of food in a common larder.

Britain's smallest mammal—and almost certainly the most active— is the pygmy shrew. This and the common shrew are frequent inhabitants of the hedge, and often occur together in the same area. Under most hedgerows, hidden to the unsuspecting eye of non-inquisitive man, is a complex and elaborate system of tunnels. Although some of these have probably been excavated by shrews, they also use the burrows made by other animals like the field mouse. The pygmy shrew, common shrew, hedgehog and mole are all insectivorous species, and a superficial search will show that there is abundant insect life in a hedgerow haunt.

With this rich fauna of small animals, birds of prey are regular visitors; sparrowhawks steadily hunt the hedgerow, the barn owl swoops silently down at dusk. Stoats and weasels may be residents or visitors; at one time rabbits were common in the hedgerows, and formed a major part of the stoat's diet. Although they are still found—locally in quantity—rabbit numbers have been drastically reduced in many areas by the endemic myxomatosis, and their predators have turned to smaller species like voles and mice.

THE BADGER (*Meles meles*)

Shy, secretive and elusive, the badger is more often present in suitable hedgebanks than most people realise. Like other members of the Mustelidae family, the badger has musk glands at the base of its tail, but unlike the weasels and stoats it does not use the liquid to leave scent-marks to indicate ownership. The musk seems to be exuded when the badgers are frightened or when playing.

Bear-like in build, a full-grown badger is about 3ft (1m) in length, with short tail and short limbs with strong claws. What it lacks in length it makes up for in power.

Until you see it at very close range, the badger's coat appears to be grey, but in fact it consists of a mixture of black and white hairs. Close to a sett on a moonlit night, when the badger quietly emerges it is the head which is its most striking feature: white, with two broad black stripes which start almost at the tip of the muzzle and go back behind the ears. Even in daylight it is difficult to see the small eyes set in the black stripes, and at night they are virtually impossible to detect.

To see a badger in daylight is a rare event, although many other nocturnal animals will be seen around from time to time. Every evening, during late spring and summer, the badgers emerge from their setts, the time varying according to weather conditions. In autumn and winter they are more regular, setting out about an hour after sunset.

There is no mistaking the badger's home site. It often chooses steep hedgebanks, where the soil is light and easily workable. The area is characterised by a number of holes, larger than those made by fox or rabbit. At the hole entrances a mass of stones and soil thrown up during the badger's burrowing activities are strewn around.

Well trodden paths around the sett indicate the badger's movements, and it is often possible to follow these. Quite often they will lead to water, perhaps a pond or stream where the badger comes for its regular drink. The familiar black-and-white hairs may be seen hanging from a strand of barbed wire or from a bramble bush, and a search around will reveal other signs of activity. Scratching posts are necessary—the bark removed from a tree reveals this. Not far from the sett, probably within 20yd (6m) or so, there will be latrines; the badger has a reputation for being particular. It is also known to change its bedding at regular intervals, and a wide variety of plant material may be found around the entrance holes. The badger collects its bedding and then, clasping it not too firmly in its front paws, it shuffles backwards to the sett, successfully installing only a proportion of it!

Once a badger has found a mate, he probably stays with her for life. The male (boar) and the female (sow) mate in July or August, and delayed implantation is a necessary feature of their reproductive cycle. the embryo does not start to develop until December or January, and in February or March the litter will be born—from one to five almost insignificant pink piglets, no more than 4 or 5in (12cm) in length.

They stay underground, fed by their mother, for six to eight weeks. By then the cubs are miniatures of their parents and can venture forth from the safety of home, with tentative, unsure first steps. The sow of course leads them out, sniffing the evening air to make sure that the coast is clear. The first few visits out of doors are short, but as the cubs gain in confidence they will stay for longer periods. Once accustomed to their new-found freedom, they will venture further away, taking each other on in simple games. Soon the female will take them for their first important lesson: how to catch their own food. By October they will be ready to leave and start a life of their own.

Threatened with danger, the badger does not run away; its first reaction is to let out a loud, weird, even wild, snorting noise—sudden and unexpected enough to scare almost any potential troublemaker. It then uses its fur to 'inflate' its stature; when the hairs bristle and stand on end, the result is a badger which appears to be almost twice its normal size: a fright indeed for an adversary.

In Yorkshire, many local people used to believe that the badger's legs were not the same length. The reason for this, they suggested, was that the foreleg on one side of the body was the same length as the hind leg on the same side. The others were shorter or longer—depending of course from which side you viewed the animal. There was, of course, a very practical reason for having 'odd' pairs of legs. It made it easier for badgers to run up and down slopes, such as hills!

The reasons for the colour pattern of the badger's coat have given rise to a number of theories, one suggesting that the striking contrast of black and white hairs is warning colouration—as shown by other animals including skunks and by smaller species like wasps and bees. But the badger does not seem to have any enemies, except man, even if we look back at some now-extinct animals which once kept company with it. Perhaps the colour helps the badger to recognise another, both in its darkened world underground and outdoors at night. Another theory, accepted in earlier days but now generally rejected, is that the colour, particularly on the striped part of the body, is like shafts of moonlight. But the badger is not particularly fond of moonlit nights, and when it does appear in moonlight it is extremely conspicuous.

BANK VOLE (*Clethrionomy glareolus*)
The bank vole, bank mouse (named after its home site) or red mouse (because of the colour of its coat) is one of the commonest rodents found in banks and hedgerows, where it shows its agility as it climbs up the hedge bushes to take ripe fruits in autumn. Provided sufficient cover is offered, it will become a hedgerow resident.

Voles are mouse-like in shape, but have a blunt muzzle and smaller eyes, and the ears are hidden by the fur. On the upper part of the body, the coat is a bright chestnut-red, with the black upper surface of the tail contrasting sharply. Underneath the colour is much lighter, anything from yellow through to buff or off-white, the latter being most common. The body is some 3.5–4in. (9–10cm) long, about half of this being tail. Peak weight of around an ounce (25–30g) is reached in summer, and this will probably be halved during the winter.

In a hedge providing dense enough cover, the bank vole's nest may be above ground, and around its territory, occupying an area of as much as 150ft (50m) or so in diameter, there will be a network of runs and tunnels. In a hedge with thinner vegetation the animal will move below the soil, having a similar nest and tunnel system.

The nest is built from grass and moss, with bark sometimes added. The bank vole breeds at any time of year from April through to October; the greatest number of births is probably in June, but if food is plentiful breeding may possibly occur in almost any other month. The young are born about eighteen days after mating and, in a good year, each female will have four or five litters, each with three to six young, so a female bank vole probably has between fifteen and thirty young, and may become pregnant again while still suckling the previous litter. The young voles are ready to leave the mother at about seventeen days and at four to five weeks old are themselves ready to breed.

Though the numbers born are so large, many of course will never reach maturity, and of those that do a high proportion will never see the following spring; only a very small percentage reach the age of two. Large numbers fall prey to the animals that scour the hedgerow regularly for food, especially to weasels, kestrels, barn owls and tawny owls. There appears to be a three- to four-year cycle, during which large populations will build up and then dwindle, leaving a scarcity for a short while. Some of the species which feed on them, and in particular the owls, seem to increase and decrease their own numbers along with the voles.

In spite of its predators, the bank vole is one of the commonest of our small mammals and very much a part of hedgerow life. Until it was described in 1832 it was thought to be a rarity—strange, since it is not particularly secretive, being found out and about during daytime, although of course it does usually remain underneath the vegetation.

A hedgerow with a wide variety of plant material will keep bank voles happily in food. They are mainly vegetarian by nature, taking a wide range of material, including bulbs, seeds, young shoots, roots, nuts and berries, but about 30 per cent of their diet consists of insects and other larvae, and they probably eat some other invertebrate animals such as snails and slugs. The vole will climb up stems to nibble the succulent new growth of, for example, hawthorn and wild rose; in autumn it will give a repeat performance (superb to watch) when seeking the hips and haws.

HEDGEHOG (*Erinaceus europaeus*)
As its name indicates, the hedgehog or hedge-pig has long been known as a hedgerow animal. The males and females (boars and sows) look alike, although the female usually measures only some 9in (24cm) to the male's 10in (27cm). The spines, sharp and pointed and about ¾in (17mm) long, grow on the top of the head and over the back, coming out at an angle from the body. The spineless parts of the body are covered with coarse hairs.

With the decrease in the amount of hedgerows, many hedgehogs have changed their habits, and seek out urban as well as suburban gardens. A well-stocked herbaceous border is in any case likely to yield as much food as some of the rather sparse hedges typical of certain areas.

As the sun goes down, and twilight creeps silently over the countryside, the nocturnal hedgehog sets forth on its night-time foraging. Although it appears to have a cumbersome body set on short legs, it gets about quickly. However, ever-conscious of impending danger, it will stop in its tracks at even the quietest sound, probably inaudible to the human ear; it draws forward the spines covering the top of its head in preparation for a complete curl-up; if in the least unsure whether the danger has passed, it will take the necessary evasive action. The soft parts of the body, the legs and the head, are withdrawn and soon the rest of the prickly coat will be pulled around them, completing its defensive system; to all intents and purposes the hedgehog becomes no more than a ball of prickles.

In many cases the hedge bottom is a suitable daytime resting place for the hedgehog, providing that there is a supply of dry leaf-litter.

Emerging at night to feed, it searches out the soft-bodied animals—slugs, worms, insects and snails—that form the major part of its diet. It will turn to other food from time to time, and snakes, lizards, frogs, rats and mice might be seized upon. It also eats some vegetable matter including berries and acorns. Some hedgehogs do take birds' eggs mainly those of ground-nesting species such as pheasant and the partridge which it comes across during its night-time jaunts.

The boars and sows mate in spring, a first litter being born in May or June after a gestation period of thirty to forty days. A second litter may be born late in summer, perhaps in August or September. The three to seven blind, deaf, helpless piglets are left to the care of the sow alone, the boar taking no interest whatsoever once mating has taken place.

At birth the young hedgehogs have a few pale-coloured spines, rubber-like in texture, and after about two days a second group of spines appears. These are darker in colour, interspersed between the earlier ones. A new piglet does not have the ability to roll into a ball; this will come when it is about ten days old, and within two weeks it will see the light of day for the first time when its eyes open. Yet another set of spines starts to appear at this time, pushing their way through the skin. These are different again from the first two sets, each one having a darker band in the middle with a lighter area on either side.

A month after birth the young piglet will be weaned and will have started taking its first indecisive yet inquisitive steps away from the safety of the nest. At about this time the first two coats of spines fall out. Although the young hedgehog will soon be ready for an independent life, it will be twelve months before it is mature and ready to breed.

Perhaps the best-known attribute of the hedgehog is its ability to pass the winter curled up in a state of hibernation. As summer comes to an end, it makes active preparations for the forthcoming resting period, carefully searching out a suitable site. Its choice of place varies; some will make their nest in a compost heap, some between the protruding roots of a large tree, and yet others in a hole in a bank; some even choose one which has previously held a colony of wasps. Having satisfied itself that its resting place will be dry, it collects together dry leaves and pieces of moss, using them to line the nest.

Hibernation does not, as most people suppose, happen suddenly. A hedgehog starts to sleep longer as days grow shorter and colder, and these inanimate periods gradually extend until the animal does not wake up. Some hedgehogs go to sleep in October and do not wake again until the following spring, but this is perhaps the exception rather than the rule; many of them will be out and about from time to time until December, and it is not particularly unusual to see them grunting and snorting their way along a hedge bottom in hopeful search for a meal when snow is on the ground, or the surrounding vegetation is covered with a layer of crisp frost. The longest sleepers appear to be older animals; younger ones do not settle down or sleep so deeply until much further into the winter.

During summer and autumn an excess of food is eaten, and that not needed by the body in its normal day-to-day activities is stored as fat. At one time this fat, brown in colour, was known as the 'hibernating gland'. This store has been found to act rather like the lining in a thermos flask, protecting the hedgehog when it most needs it, during its period of relative inactivity. During its winter's sleep its body activities slow down so that much less energy is needed. The heartbeat in hibernating hedgehogs is difficult to detect and breathing is very slow. These processes are at such a low level that they draw off only small amounts of energy, obtained from the stored fat.

As a common English animal, the hedgehog has featured widely in folklore for a very long time. At one time it was thought capable of predicting the weather:

> Observe which way the hedgehog builds its nest
> To front the north or south, or east or west,
> For if 'tis true that common people say,
> The wind will blow the quite contrary way.
> If by some secret art the hedgehog know
> So long before which way the wind will blow,
> She has an art which many a person lacks,
> That himself thinks fit to make almanacks.

164

This appeared in *Poor Robin's Almanack*, in 1733!

Two of the most popular beliefs held by country people were that, first, the hedgehog would roll on fallen apples, thus collecting them on its spines, and second that it sucked milk from cows' udders. Indeed until quite recently hedgehogs were worth money; each had a bounty on its head, and many churchwardens' accounts show that payments were made to people who caught them: their sin was this alleged sucking of milk from cows! As so often, there is a gleam of truth in the story. When cows are at rest in a field, hedgehogs are occasionally seen around the animals' udders, looking for insects; naturally hedgehogs are partial to milk, and if they found milk oozing from a leaking teat, they would take the opportunity to lick it up. Although countrymen's reports are viewed with much scepticism by naturalists who know the behaviour of the animal, nevertheless in an experiment carried out in 1968 a hedgehog seized an artificial teat without a second bidding and drained it dry! Farmers also claim that hedgehogs will damage cows' teats with their spines. They say that the damage only appears from late spring to early autumn, when the hedgehogs are abroad, and so again they are blamed.

The idea that the hedgehog impales apples on its spines was written down by Edward Topsell in the seventeenth century, in his *History of Foure Footed Beastes*. He indicated that 'when he findeth apples or grapes on the earth he rowleth himselfe uppon them, untill he have filled all his prickles . . .', and went on to explain that as the hedgehog moved so he sounded like a 'carte wheele'. But this idea goes back much further: there are manuscripts and pieces of pottery produced more than two thousand years ago which show hedgehogs with fruits attached to their spines.

LONG-TAILED FIELD MOUSE (*Apodemus sylvaticus*)
The long-tailed field mouse is common in hedgerows or woods—its other name is wood mouse. About 6½ to 7in long (16 to 17cm), of which half is tail, the field mouse weighs in at about ¼ of an ounce (7g). Its eyes and ears are large, the latter well back on the head. The white fur underneath the body contrasts with the bright fawn on the upper parts, broken by a yellow patch on the chest, and sometimes by yellow

streaks on the flanks. The hind legs are noticeably longer than the forelegs.

Where a hedgerow provides food and cover, the field mouse will be usually found there. In among the leaf litter, the animal will make a bewildering network of tunnels. Like the bank vole, if the ground cover is not sufficient, it will move below the soil. The extensive underground system is only revealed by its entrances, holes about 1½in (4cm) across. Small cairns, about 2in (5cm) high, have sometimes been found close to these holes, but no one has yet been able to explain them. Strangely, after a while, the stones have been discovered scattered over a wide area away from the entrance holes. If humans purposely remove the stones, they will be collected up again and the cairn rebuilt.

Although their greatest period of activity is at night, field mice are sometimes out and about during the hours of daylight. Some naturalists have suggested that the animal is colonial, the groups being based on the family unit.

Even when mice are above-ground dwellers, the nest, made from grass collected and finely shredded, is usually below the surface. Sometimes the mice will take over birds' nests, and these may even be several feet above the ground. In the nest, after a gestation period of about twenty-five days, the female gives birth to up to five litters a year, each of which may have up to six young. They are fed by the mother for three weeks, and about a fortnight after birth can leave the nest for short periods. It is reckoned that those that survive will be ready to breed at about five months.

Predators coming to the hedge for food will find a plentiful supply of these prolific breeders. Owls, the tawny in particular, along with the fierce little carnivores, the stoats and weasels, will scour the hedgerow for them; foxes will take many, and even common crows are partial to young ones.

The long-tailed field mouse, like its relatives, is a hoarder. As soon as a good supply of food, such as acorns, is available, it collects together a store. If the nuts are removed and scattered over an area of something in the region of a quarter-acre the mice set to work to retrieve them and within a matter of hours all will be safely gathered in, apart of course from any seized by other hungry animals. Disused birds' nests

make favourite larders, those of blackbirds and linnets being particularly favoured, perhaps not surprisingly considering their frequency
along the hedgerow. Those fairly low in the hedge are preferred.
Sitting on the edge of the nest, the mouse will take its fill, almost
meticulously putting the waste which it finds unpalatable back into
the nest, among the store of uneaten food! This activity was recorded
by Mary Hewitt back in 1843:

> In the hedge sparrow's nest he sits,
> When its summer brood is fled,
> And picks the berries from the bough
> Of the hawthorn overhead.

The variety of food taken depends on the mouse concerned. It is
known that juveniles prefer fungi and nuts, in consequence taking
fewer insects than the older animals. Males tend to eat large numbers
of nuts, whereas females are attracted to vegetation. All in all the
variety is wide, and includes snails, fungi, insects, grain, nuts, acorns,
fruits, buds, seeds and seedlings, according to what is most available.
With fruits like the hawthorn, the mouse opens them out, throws away
the fleshy part and takes out the seeds. These are then broken open,
the material inside eaten, and the seed cases then disposed of.

Like bank voles, field mice will climb up the hedge for fruits or
shoots they like; in some hedges they will live largely on hips and
haws in autumn.

MOLE (*Talpa europaea*)
A woodland and grassland dweller by nature, the mole has had to
adapt to changing conditions, such as the ever more active management
of pastureland. Now large numbers are recorded in hedgerows, used
as the starting point before food-hunting forays into ploughed fields
and grassland.

Destined for a life of almost total darkness, below the surface of the
soil, the mole is well adapted to its role of underground excavator. Its
cylindrical body terminates in a long pointed snout, and at the other
end with a club-shaped tail. Its eyes, unnecessary in its dark under-

ground world, are small and almost hidden in its velvety dark-grey or black fur. The need to see has gone, and the mole is almost blind. But what it lacks by way of sight, it makes up for with well-developed senses of hearing and smell. In addition, the whiskers on the snout and head are extremely sensitive. The mole also seems to be able to 'pick up' sounds which occur at a distance.

Its forelimbs have evolved to fit a life spent digging underground —set forward on the body, broad and facing outwards. The strong forefeet are in complete contrast to the weak hind limbs and do the tunnelling work. To start with the mole loosens the soil and then, using its feet as shovels, pushes it backwards. The hind feet are used to help push the animal forward in a combination of swimming and loping movements.

Although so little of the mole's activity can be watched, it is a restless and hard-working creature, its digging and feeding sometimes going on for upwards of four-and-a-half hours, in what appear to be almost frenzied attacks on the soil in front of it. Having worked and fed for this time, the mole must be exhausted, and for the next three-and-a-half hours it will rest. Only short visits are made to the world above ground. The signs of mole activity are the piles of soil on the surface of the field or the hedgebank (or your lawn): the unmistakeable mole-hills. These are the spoil heaps of excavated soil pushed up as the mole busies away underground.

It has two types of underground runs. Working just below the surface it will push up a ridge of soil as it moves along. In addition there is a permanent network of underground tunnels. Some $2\frac{1}{2}$ to $5\frac{1}{2}$in (7 to 14cm) below the surface, these run horizontally through the soil with a further system 6in (15cm) below this. From the bottom system vertical if somewhat erratic shafts are dug to a depth of between 3–4ft (1–1.5m).

At one time country people suggested that moles had fortresses. This idea arose because moles sometimes excavate part of a tunnel to form a nest, lined with twigs, leaves or grass, and surround it with getaway tunnels, providing almost limitless means of escape. Sometimes the nests, where the moles rest between their periods of vigorous digging, may be as deep as 3ft (1m) below the soil; sometimes they may be at the surface, when the 'fortress' will be clearly visible, surrounded with a mound of soil anything up to 3ft (1m) high and 9½ft (2.5m) across.

Males (boars) and females (sows) live independent lives, only coming together towards the end of March or early in April to mate. Five to six weeks after conception a litter of two to seven blind, pink, naked young will be born. Fur starts to appear after two weeks, and in another eight days the eyes will open, although what the animals see will be strictly limited. Thirty-five days after birth, the young are ready to leave the mother. It is at this time that the moles are most vulnerable and only a small percentage of the youngsters will ultimately reach sexual maturity in the following spring. At this stage, when they spend more time at or above the surface, they fall prey to a wide variety of enemies, including weasels, stoats, badgers, herons, owls and foxes.

The relentless digging is associated with the constant search for food: moles must feed almost continuously. Unless they do, they will die. The maximum possible period without food is probably indicated by the rests of about three and a half hours.

Nor surprisingly, seeing where it lives, the major part of the mole's diet is usually made up of earthworms. When there are plenty it will often form a store. To immobilise the worm, it first bites off the segments at the head end, and then ties the remaining part into a knot. These worms are then stored in the larder. The mole is a hoarder, and larders holding more than 100 earthworms have been found. The worm supply is usually adequate and the prudent stand-by store is often not needed: having been left for some time the worms will often grow a new head and then make off.

The mole also encounters other suitable food, including wireworms and leatherjackets. An earthworm diet gives all the water a mole needs: of a worm's body about four-fifths is water.

The mole gets its name from the Anglo-Saxon 'mouldewarp', 'mould turner'. As a common countryside mammal, it featured in folklore. Blood taken from the animal's nose and placed on a lump of sugar was the suggested remedy for anyone suffering from fits. A specimen in the museum at Scarborough, bearing the date 1911, shows how earlier folk revered the mole: one of the animal's claws is wrapped in a silken cloth—carried around it was said to stop cramp. If a mole was captured and its foot cut off while it was still alive, this was supposed to cure toothache.

Other country beliefs are from Scotland. If a mole appeared in the grounds of a house, and encircled the building with its underground tunnels, a death was almost curtain. If it simply continued burrowing close to the house, it was a sign that the inhabitants would move away.

RABBIT (*Oryctolagus cuniculus*)
Until the rabbit was almost wiped out with virulent myxomatosis, it was almost certainly the commonest hedgerow mammal, its population reaching huge numbers, even plague proportions, in some areas. The rabbit is not a native of the British Isles, and there has naturally been disagreement as to who was responsible for its introduction.

Originally the Romans were blamed, then later the Normans. Other naturalists suggest that it was not brought here until the twelfth century. In any case it was brought in for food and for sport. It used to be farmed for food, breeding in warrens, particularly in areas of poor, light soils in East Anglia.

Like the hedgehog, the rabbit is universally known, regularly seen playing and grazing in fields at early morning and in the evening. Rounded, furry and endearing, he is Peter Rabbit, the children's favourite—whatever destruction he may wreak on crops. A fairly defenceless animal, the rabbit relies on fast retreat to its burrow if a predator appears. Its large eyes, placed well to the side of the head, allow a wide range of vision, and its long ears 'trap' sounds. Long, powerful back legs give fast bursts of speed. These legs are also used to thump the ground in a frenzied attempt to warn other rabbits when danger is detected.

The coat is made of three types of hairs, which account for its almost mottled appearance. The fur closest to the skin is soft and downy, and obviously has good insulating qualities. Projecting through this are longer hairs, which give the brownish colour, and the third type of hair, less evenly distributed, is longer than the other two and gives extra protection in winter. The rabbit's short tail has white hairs underneath—the familiar white scut so conspicuous when a rabbit dashes off for shelter.

Although males (bucks) and females (does) appear alike from a distance, the does have slightly longer faces, and the bucks are larger and heavier, measuring up to 15-16in (40cm) in length, with a weight of about 4-4½lb (2kg).

Rabbits mark their territories with a secretion produced by glands under the chin, these being larger and more pronounced in the male than in the female. The secretion is also used to mark other rabbits: a buck may rub his chosen mate, or a female may mark her young.

Originally a native of grassland and woods, with the vast amount of hedgerow which appeared, particularly at the time of the Enclosures and with diminishing woodland, the rabbit has taken to the hedge. On agricultural land laid down with crops or offering good grass and herbage, this provides suitable living quarters with a seemingly never-decreasing food source nearby. At the height of their population success, before being stricken with myxomatosis, they did many millions of pounds' worth of damage to farm crops. Today, local populations are still high in places and they still cause consternation to the farmer, devouring tons of precious foodstuffs. Almost totally vegetarian, the rabbit turns to the bark of trees in winter when green-stuff is scarce, and can cause havoc in orchards or forestry plantations. Although mainly feeding at night, it may be seen at any time.

In suitable hedgebanks, the rabbit will live, breed and feed. To construct its system of underground tunnels, it loosens the soil with its forepaws and pushes it back with its hindpaws. The diameter of each tunnel is usually about 6in (15cm), and because rabbits are highly social animals and numbers of them often occupy each underground home, the tunnel must be widened at intervals so that the animals can pass each other. At a selected spot along one of the main tunnels, the rabbit will excavate a resting nest. There is only one exit, leading to the main tunnel.

Once a buck has his eye on a doe, he will chase her in a courtship ritual. A litter will be born within twenty-eight days of mating, the first babies of the year usually appearing in January, and each doe producing several more batches between then and June. Some breeding occurs during the rest of the year. A buck will usually mate with a number of does, but each female keeps her own particular part of the underground home, not intruding into another's territory.

Once pregnant, the female prepares a suitable birthplace for the young, keeping well away from the main tunnel because the bucks are likely to kill newly born offspring. She excavates a short chamber, a 'stop' or blind burrow, usually less than 3ft (1m) long and probably just below the surface.

Two to eight babies are born, numbers tending to increase as the weather gets warmer. At birth the young rabbits are helpless, almost completely naked, blind and deaf. For about ten days they remain almost immobile in the nest, only searching for the female's teats when she comes to feed them. On the eleventh day the eyes will open, and in about a month they will be weaned, having learned to forage for themselves. Until they are ready to leave, the female is an exceptionally protective mother and using her powerful rear legs will do all she can to keep predators from the very vulnerable young ones. But weasels, stoats and foxes kill off a sizeable number before they reach sexual maturity, and at three months or so are ready to breed themselves.

During her rearing period the doe only leaves the stop for a few minutes in every twenty-four-hour period. When she goes, she makes sure that the young are well protected by filling in the stop, and as an extra precaution she will even spread leaves over the surface to 'hide' the soil.

Not only the young out at play are in danger. Badgers will actually dig into a nest for the young, and foxes and stoats also do this. Outside, these carnivores are joined by birds of prey, such as owls and buzzards, and by predators such as crows and ravens, and domestic cats and dogs.

With the onslaught of the highly infectious myxomatosis epidemic in 1954 and 1955, which virtually wiped out complete rabbit populations in some areas, the plants usually nibbled down along hedgerows and verges suddenly grew up into new prominence. Then, as the disease appeared to abate, the rabbit population started to recover, only to be struck by another outbreak. There is evidence now that in some places rabbits have developed resistance to it, and certainly numbers have risen substantially.

SHREW (*Sorex araneus* and *S. minutus*)

Common and pygmy shrews are both found in our hedgerows (though only the pygmy in Ireland). The pygmy has the distinction of being the smallest of Britain's mammals. Resembling a mouse in general appearance, shrews are characterised by their long tapering snouts, small eyes and ears and soft fur—a dingy white under the body and varying from grey to dark brown on top.

The shrew's overriding activity is to find food. Because of its small bulk compared with the quite large surface area it loses body heat at a much greater rate than some larger animals and must work hard to replace this—and all the energy lost in doing so. Its whole lifestyle is a vicious circle. Each day follows a three-hourly rhythm: the shrew feeds continuously for three hours, and then rests for the next three hours. If it is unable to obtain food every three hours or so, it will die. When the temperature falls, eating must be even more frequent. During autumn and winter many shrews literally 'drop dead'. Having spent some of the time feeding, they will rest, and then without warning die; a condition brought about by 'cold starvation'.

The breeding season spans the period from spring through to autumn, and each fertile female will produce two litters of four to eight young, born in a loosely woven grass nest. About three weeks after birth the eyes are opened, and a few days later the young are no longer dependent on their mother.

Although shrews have some form of defence in that their glands produce an unpleasant liquid, enough to keep some enemies at bay, large numbers, the young in particular, fall to predators, especially owls, weasels and stoats.

Shrews are solitary by nature, living in grass runs, amongst dead-leaf litter or even under the ground. They seldom come out into the open, although their whereabouts can generally be pinpointed with reasonable accuracy from their high-pitched squeaks.

People have believed that shrews are 'vicious' animals, and certainly when picked up they are always ready to snap out with their sharp teeth. As befits animals which live in a solitary state, they are naturally cautious about intrusions, even when these come from their own kind. They were thought to be irritable and quarrelsome; however, as with

173

other aspects of animal behaviour, detailed study leads to more understanding of the whys and wherefores.

Recently it has been discovered that when shrews meet they view each other with great caution, moving forward until their whiskers, the sensitive vibrissae on their snouts used when finding food, actually come into contact. Having established contact they start to squeak and the intruding animal usually beats a hasty retreat. If it does not, both animals will then stand on their hind legs, the squeaking continuing unabated. If this method of attack does not work, both will throw themselves on to their backs, wriggling in an apparent frenzy, with the squeaking reaching a new pitch. During the combat, the muzzle of one latches onto the tail of the other, an action quickly taken up by the second shrew. Locked together their struggle continues, but in spite of uninformed country tales, injury seldom occurs. When it does, it is minor. Such attacks are thought to be self-protective behaviour, each shrew needing to keep its own established territory in order to guard its food supply.

Although shrews mainly eat insects, they seize almost anything available—worms, snails and carrion, and also a lot of vegetable matter, mostly seeds.

For all its familiarity, the shrew's life and habits are not well understood, and the myths and legends around it have not helped. One strange story is that if shrews cross a human path they will die. This myth has been reinforced by the fact that over the years a number of people have seen shrews moving towards them in what appears to be a drunken state; and on reaching the human's feet they have 'dropped dead'. There are two rational explanations for this: either the animal could have been suffering from cold starvation, or it could have been old and ready to die anyway. The fact that it happened at a person's feet was purely coincidental, unless an element of fright helped to finish it off.

10

The Smaller Inhabitants

The lush, succulent growth within the hedgerow attracts a wide range of invertebrate animals—those without backbones, the insects, spiders slugs, snails, worms and others. Hedge plants provide food directly for some of them, indirectly for others. And as these small creatures come for their fill, to nectar-laden flowers, green leaves or ripe berries, they in their turn provide a meal for innumerable other species ever watching for food.

A world of wildlife can be watched on the flower heads and munching the fruits or leaves; another tribe, unseen, is quietly searching for food in the hedge bottom. Here is an accumulation of debris which fell from the herbaceous plants of the year before as well as from the trees and shrubs. Stems and twigs fall to add to the rich rubbish and gradually rot away, putting back into the soil some of the nutrients they absorbed when living. For hedge-bottom creatures, food, shelter and relative safety are available.

By far the greatest number of the animals living in, or visiting hedgerows are invertebrates. Although not one solitary bird's nest may be found, in a 20yd (18m) stretch of well-established mixed hedge, at least one hundred *different* invertebrate species would be likely. These creatures are often unnoticed by the casual observer; but not by the mammals and birds which rely on them for food.

Many kinds of butterflies, such as the small tortoiseshell, red admiral and peacock, to name the most conspicuously decorative, seek out hedgerow plants for nectar and for egg-laying. The situation of the hedge of course to some extent determines the plant species it contains and thereby the moths and butterflies that come to it. These, after all, are only there for one of the two purposes just mentioned, and if there are no nectar-yielding flowers, and the right food plants on which to lay their eggs are absent, then the hedge is no help to them. Butterflies finding nourishment from the hedge flowers will also lay their eggs there if possible.

None of the butterflies found in the British Isles can be truly labelled a 'hedge' species, though perhaps the hedge brown (or gatekeeper), a lover of bramble blossom, is found here more frequently than in any other habitat. Nevertheless the hedgerow, particularly where it borders a verge with a plentiful supply of grasses and other herbage, is important for butterflies. It provides many of the plants needed by our commoner species, such as the orange tip, meadow brown and green-veined white, as well as the beautiful Vanessids already listed. For other species too, although they may breed in different habitats, it is valuable: as for birds, it acts as a corridor between sections of countryside, linking one area of woodland with another, allowing the butterflies to move into new areas for feeding and breeding. It provides shelter and, depending on its orientation, may be enough of a suntrap to provide particularly good conditions for the development of eggs.

The commonest hedge shrub, the hawthorn, is an extremely valuable food for butterfly and moth larvae. As already said, entomologists have estimated that at least one hundred species of moth caterpillars feed on hawthorn shoots in the spring and early summer. One of the other plants valuable to moths and a common hedgerow shrub in some parts of the country is blackthorn.

The effects of new hedge-management methods on invertebrate populations are much debated. Some of these creatures have undoubtedly decreased in numbers in recent years. An example is the small eggar moth (*Eriogaster lanestris*). Its larvae are gregarious, feeding on hawthorn in compact nests. Early in the year, the exact time depending on weather conditions, the adults emerge and the eggs are laid in close batches on the terminal twigs of hawthorn in February or early March. It is possible that the small eggar may have fallen victim to a virus, something that does happen to gregarious species, but it seems more likely that hedge-management techniques, such as regular mechanical trimming, are responsible.

Local authorities have largely abandoned using herbicides on roadside verges; but they and the hedges are cut at regular intervals, even if the frequency and severity of mechanical trimming sessions have decreased. In certain areas, especially where hedges occur between fields and away from roads, the butterflies and moths will not be so much disturbed. Against this, the number and variety of plants growing in these situations is often poorer than along roadside verges, largely because of the use of weedkillers on the nearby field crops. Larvae are also at risk from farmers' pesticides.

Hedges which are proving extremely useful wildlife habitats are those alongside closed country railway lines. Many of these deserted tracks are to all intents and purposes inaccessible and undisturbed, and they have helped to replace the sanctuaries lost when great tracts of hedgerow have been grubbed up elsewhere.

Butterflies

The butterflies which lay their eggs on hedgerow plants, whether or not exclusively, may need particular kinds of trees or bushes, or they may solely use some of the wide range of grasses which grow so profusely in many hedgerows and their adjacent verges. Grass-feeders include the wall brown, the hedge brown, the meadow brown, various skippers, the ringlet, the small heath and the speckled wood. Nine or so species rely extensively on other non-woody hedgerow plants, most using only one particular plant or family of plants. The small copper's eggs and larvae will be found on sorrel and dock, the small white, the green-veined white and the orange tip often feed on jack-by-the-hedge and other cruciform species, brimstones rely on buckthorn, the green hairstreak on either gorse or bird's-foot trefoil. The common blue uses members of the clover family, including bird's-foot trefoil as well as clover itself. Peacock and small tortoiseshell come here to lay on nettles. All these butterflies, together with the large white, painted lady and red admiral, will come to the hedge to feed. Here are descriptions of a few of the butterflies found in or near any mixed hedge:

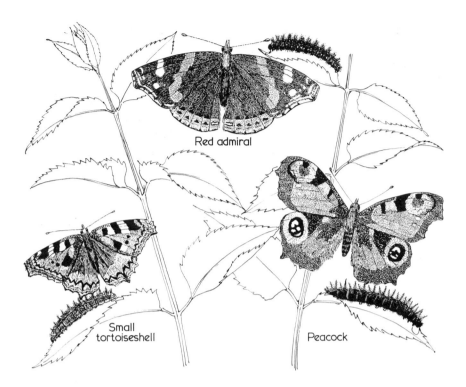

Red admiral

Small
tortoiseshell

Peacock

HEDGE BROWN (*Pyronia tithonus*)

Flitting around country lanes, never straying far from the hedgerow, as its name implies, the hedge brown is found over much of southern England, being one of our commonest butterflies. Its other name is gatekeeper, reflecting its liking for hedgerows, verges and the borders of woodlands. In a particularly good season it can still be seen on the wing in large numbers, although it has decreased in recent years. Much less frequent in the north of England, it does not occur in Scotland.

The female, larger than the male, generally has brighter reddish-yellow markings on the upper side of the otherwise brown wings. There is a wide variety of colouration, and albinos are not unknown.

The first butterflies emerge towards the end of July and they will be on the wing during the coming months. The female lays her primrose-yellow eggs singly on blades of grass. Once the caterpillars have emerged, within a few days providing that weather conditions are suitable, they will feed on grass until late in the summer. Then they will hibernate and stay in this state for around eight months. Not fully fed when they go into hibernation, they will awake around the middle of March and resume their interrupted feeding. Slow, even sluggish, as they move about they feed in leisurely fashion. During the daytime they will be safely out of sight, deep in the grass tussocks, coming out at night to feed.

LARGE AND SMALL WHITES (*Pieris brassicae* and *P. rapae*)
Both large and small whites search out the leaves of plants belonging to the *Cruciferae* family, on which they will ultimately lay their eggs. They, like other butterflies, are able to detect the food plant for their caterpillars by its scent. Although we associate these butterflies, and particularly the large white, with devastating our carefully cultivated green vegetables, including the cabbage, they are often found on wild *Cruciferae* in the hedge, including the hedge mustard.

Occurring almost anywhere in the British Isles, the numbers fluctuating from year to year, the whites will first be seen on the wing in April or May. Since both species over-winter as chrysalids, the exact time of emergence will depend on prevailing weather conditions.

Female large whites lay their eggs in untidy, irregular groups, on the lower surface of the leaves. The small white is rather more particular, siting hers singly on the under-surface, and will spread them over a wide area, on many different plants.

The caterpillars of the large white remain together when they first hatch, and only chew the surface of the leaf. After their first moult, however, they seem to acquire greater energy, and will now eat through the leaf. Several caterpillars may be seen arranged around the edge of a fresh leaf, moving backwards as they consume it. After feeding together for some time, and when about two-thirds grown, they split up and feed singly. When ready to pupate they either cling to the stems of their food plant, or go off to find a gate, fence or wall. Many will never pupate, because a parasitic ichneumon fly, *Apantales glomeratus*, often lays its eggs inside the caterpillar's body. Quite often

179

the dying caterpillars can be seen surrounded by yellow cocoons made by the fly.

Once the caterpillars of the small white emerge, they feed on the leaves of the host plant, making holes in the surface. So well camouflaged is the green caterpillar that even when fully grown it is seldom possible to distinguish it from the surface colour of its leaf. When resting, it will lie close to the veins on the under surface of the leaf.

The female large white is distinguished from the male by its black wing spots. Both sexes have black margins to the fore wings. The female small white has two wing spots, the male only one.

MEADOW BROWN (*Maniola jurtina*)
The meadow brown is found all over Britain except at high altitudes, and it is the commonest species of all. Like the hedge brown it is a visitor to the hedgerow because it enjoys the sheltered conditions, and can usually find plenty of food for itself and the grasses which its caterpillars will need for food.

The female lays her eggs on any of a wide range of different grasses, on which the caterpillars are very well camouflaged, taking on an almost identical shade of green. On hatching they first eat the egg case. Just before they pupate, they spin silken pads which are attached to the grass stems and suspend themselves from these, downwards. It will cast the larval skin, to which it remains attached, and will spend the next month or so in the pupal state, a longer period than most other butterflies which hatch at this time of year.

The meadow brown passes the winter in the caterpillar stage, not properly hibernating but slowing activity during cold weather. The butterfly probably never strays far from its place of birth; it is first seen on the wing in June and continues into August. It flies with a slow, almost floppy action, seldom attaining much height or speed; apparently exhausted by even the shortest flight routine, it frequently settles on herbage to rest.

RED ADMIRAL (*Vanessa atalanta*)
Although large numbers of red admiral butterflies are hatched in our country each year, few if any survive the winter. Alternate periods of

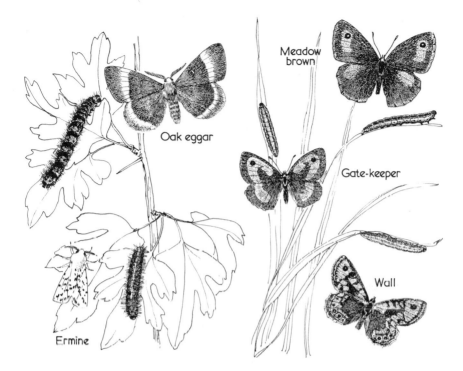

Meadow brown

Oak eggar

Gate-keeper

Wall

Ermine

cold and damp are killers. Fortunately large numbers usually reach our shores from overseas, the first generally arriving in May, others taking up residence until as late as September.

Once here the butterflies mate, and then the female seeks out the food plant, so that she can carry out the urgent task of laying her eggs, a sadly pointless operation in her case. Red admirals, like small tortoise-shells and peacocks, only lay their eggs on the leaves of stinging nettles and we can usually expect to find caterpillars on suitable patches of those in the hedgerow—usually young plants, and situated in a slight dip. Fresh new leaves will provide the most succulent food for the developing caterpillars.

The eggs are placed singly on the upper surface of the leaves, and on hatching the caterpillars make it their first task to bind together the edges of their own leaf so that they are protected within the fold, safe from predators. Once they have taken all the nourishment from one leaf they move to another, repeating this until they are fully grown. Then each one draws together a number of leaves to form a kind of tent, and suspends itself head downwards, making the change from larva to pupa inside.

Although some adults may start to make the journey back to the Mediterranean, the winter haunt of their ancestors, it is unlikely they will reach their destination. Like those that remain in Britain, they will almost certainly perish.

SMALL TORTOISESHELL (*Aglais urticae*)
Certainly one of the commonest butterflies of the countryside, occurring in a wide variety of habitats, the small tortoiseshell overwinters as a chrysalis and the survivors are among the first butterflies we see

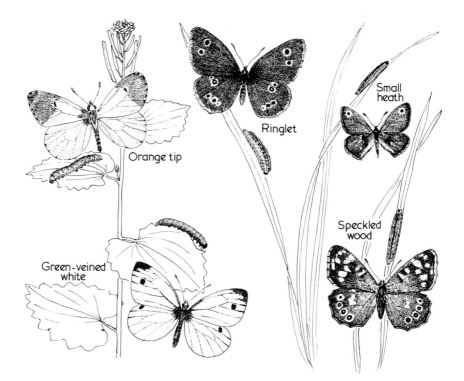

Orange tip

Ringlet

Small heath

Green-veined white

Speckled wood

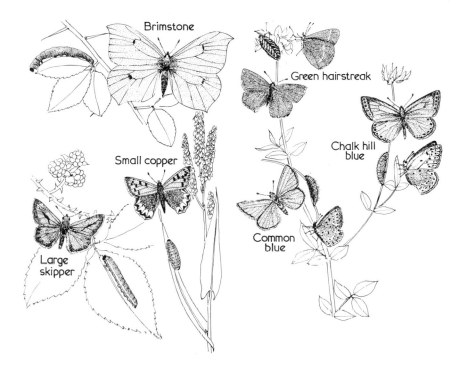

Brimstone

Green hairstreak

Chalk hill blue

Small copper

Common blue

Large skipper

on the wing in spring, as early as March or April, depending on the weather. The first larvae of the year will usually have pupated and be flying by June.

The female lays anything between fifty and a hundred pale-green eggs on the under-surface of stinging-nettle leaves growing in a suitable patch, often in a hedgerow; shortish stems are chosen or plants growing in a depression in the ground. Once emerged from the eggs, the first job of the young caterpillars is to spin a communal web over the top of the nettle plant, and secure inside they start to feed on the enclosed leaves. When new leaves are needed, they spin another web. During the daytime, when feeding ceases, the larvae use the web as a suitable site for basking in the sun. At night, and in bad weather, the web provides a useful shelter.

When almost fully grown the caterpillars separate, sometimes into small groups but more often each will live within its own folded leaf.

Usually when ready to pupate the caterpillar leaves the nettle, seeking out twigs and sticks from which to suspend itself, and there is no shortage of these along a hedgerow. An occasional caterpillar suspends itself from the nettle on which it is feeding and pupates there. The second brood emerge as adults towards the end of August, and remain on the wing until October, when they seek somewhere to hibernate in sheds, outbuildings and houses.

Male and female small tortoiseshells are similar in appearance, except that the latter seems to be slightly larger and not surprisingly tends to be seen around the nettle beds on which she will lay her eggs.

Grasshoppers

The poisonous sprays used on fields may well have decreased the grasshopper population; their incessant noise, once so familiar, seems less frequent than it was ten or so years ago, though in some localities there are still plenty. The hedgerow is still an important habitat for these insects, particularly when there is plenty of grass. Grasshoppers have short antennae; crickets have long, threadlike ones. Most of those found in our hedgerows and fields are true, short-horned grasshoppers.

With most grasshoppers species it is the male who does the 'singing'. He rubs the inside of his long hind legs, studded with about ninety little pegs, against the inside of the thickened veins on the forewings; the vibrations produce the noise. Many animals which can make sounds also have some form of hearing organ; the short-horned grasshoppers have primitive ears on each side of the abdomen.

After mating, the female starts to lay her eggs in August, and may go on doing so into September. Using the ovipositor—an egg-laying tube—she makes a hole in or under a grass tuft and in due course deposits thirty to a hundred eggs in it. She then pours a liquid over them which hardens into a waterproof covering, an egg-pod—very necessary because the eggs remain in the ground until the following May. She may dig several holes in the course of a number of weeks.

Once the young nymphs have emerged from the eggs they feed on plants, and as they grow quickly they need to shed their skin several times. Although resembling their parents at birth, they did not have

184

wings: these can be seen after they have moulted for the third time. By July they will have reached adult size.

Grasshoppers of course move mainly by hopping (though all except the meadow grasshopper can also fly). The long hind legs have powerful thighs, visibly swollen with muscles, with which they can hop a long way. The two pairs of wings are folded along the back, the first of these, known as the elytra, being horny; the second, more delicate, pair are safely folded underneath the elytra.

Spiders

It would hardly be right to look at hedgerow dwellers without considering the universally distributed spiders. Although they are generally abundant all the year round, their activities become particularly conspicuous from September through the autumn. Perhaps the only thing in the countryside more beautiful than their dew-encrusted webs glinting in the early autumn sunlight is those same miraculous pieces of craftsmanship covered with rime.

The garden (or cross, or diadem) spider (*Araneus diadematus*) is the most often seen. It is just as much at home in the hedgerow as amongst the plants in the garden. The female, a large brown or yellowish spider with a white cross on her back, builds the large web and then lies motionless, head-downwards, in its centre waiting for her prey to strike; when not in the web she lurks nearby in the privacy of some sheltered corner, connected to the web by a 'signal' thread. If an insect flounders in, the vibrations bring her chasing up to the centre and then out along a radiating strand to the victim.

To deal with their prey, spiders have fangs linked to a small bag of poison located behind the jaw. When the spider sinks its fang into an insect struggling in the web, the poison flows down a small channel to the end of the fang and enters the body of the prey which, depending on the size of species concerned, will either be paralysed or killed.

The male garden spider is less easy to discover, because he is much smaller and seldom makes webs; with or without a web, however, he may be seen near the female during the mating season, usually in September. The female lays the eggs in autumn, and wraps them in a cocoon of pale-yellow silk, which is left in a safe place until the following spring, when the young will hatch—miniature replicas of their parents. As they grow they moult their skins a number of times.

Silk for the spider's web comes from spinnerets on the underside of the female's body. Her site selected, she makes a framework of threads, stretching others across these. Sticky threads are now added: when first laid they are completely covered with a thick layer of tacky material, but before she finally secures each one, she pulls it slightly and then lets it go. The result is that the glue-like liquid is redistributed in a series of blobs. At the centre of the web she builds herself a platform of non-sticky strands.

Once prey is bitten and subdued, the spider sucks out the contents of the body, or else wraps it in silk threads to eat later. Starting with one strand, she flicks it over and over until the corpse is completely covered. Quite often these silken food parcels can be seen in the garden spider's web.

Wasps

Nests of the common wasp (*Vespula vulgaris* and *V. germanica*) are often to be found on hedge banks. Each pregnant queen wasp hibernates in some sheltered spot and emerges, large and somewhat sluggish in movement, with warmer weather as early as March or perhaps as late as the end of May. After a long period spent looking for a suitable site she starts what seems a most laborious and time-consuming activity—the building of the nest.

Having located suitable wood, she will use her strong jaws—mandibles—to pull off a strip. This is rolled up, carried to the nest site and mixed with saliva to form what is known as 'wasp paper', a brown-coloured brittle material. She fixes each piece to the roof of what is to be the nest, starting from the top and working downwards, so that the roof is literally suspended. A comb is constructed inside the golf ball-sized nest; the prime intention at this stage is to provide enough cells to take her eggs. As each cell in the comb is completed she lays an egg inside it, fixing it with a glue-like substance.

When the larvae hatch, the queen's time is divided between feeding them with pieces of fly and continuing the important nest-building operation. When ready to pupate, each larva spins a silken sheet to seal the end of its cell. About five weeks after the queen laid the egg a fully grown wasp will eventually bite its way out.

These are the worker wasps, females like the queen but much smaller. The queen is now relieved of her duties as the workers spend their time searching for food and expanding the nest. They build on many new cells, and the queen now takes to full-time egg-laying. The workers care for the larvae as they hatch out, and of course the population of the nest increases almost daily; it may eventually contain as many as 5,000 individuals and be football-size.

August is an important month in the nest, for at this time the males —drones—and young queens leave the nest and mate, to ensure that there will be pregnant queens to hibernate through the winter, ready to repeat the cycle the following season. Once the mating game is over, the queens will go in search of suitable winter quarters, and the males die.

The task over, the workers kill and eat any remaining larvae, make sure that the nest is destroyed and leave it; soon they too meet their deaths in the cold, damp autumn weather. The old queen also dies.

Molluscs

The hedge bottom is an excellent habitat for snails and slugs. Snail shells are familiar to all of us; slugs have no visible shell, though in fact there is a vestige of one on the inside in many species. These molluscs go silently about their lives, often unseen; like many species of invertebrates they must remain moist, and they find damp quarters deep down in the hedgerow where the mass of tangled vegetation is seldom warmed to any great degree by the sun's rays. Once a shower of rain has dampened the hedgerow plants, the molluscs' area of patrol increases considerably, and they can be seen climbing up and over the plants, often several feet above ground level.

The garden snail (*Helix aspersa*), with its striped brown shell, is equally at home in the hedgerow. So is the grove or brown-lipped snail, *Cepaea nemoralis*, and the prickly snail, *Acanthinula aculeata*. The shell, which looks so cumbersome, is a snail's very life-support system. It can quickly withdraw into it when threatened and in periods when the temperature is either too hot or too cold it can spend a period of quiet inactivity there. Winter hibernation may go on for several months, the shell opening sealed into an 'epiphragm' of mucus, thicker than is used for summer rests.

As the snail grows it adds to the shell: on the average snail with a shell width and height of about 1in (2.5cm), there will be about five whorls, the largest being the outer one. Shell growth proceeds slowly throughout most of the year, but stops during the dead of winter. On some shells it is possible to distinguish stronger cross-ridges which mark the termination of the preceding year's shell growth.

The flat under-surface of the snail's body is known as the foot; it is muscular and as ripples pass from one end of it to the other, the snail moves over the ground; often it leaves behind a trail of slime, which eases the animal's movement over a wide variety of surfaces.

Snails have four tentacles, a longer pair rising from the top of the head and smaller ones lower down. Both sets are sensory organs, enabling the snail to feel its surroundings, and can be withdrawn into the body: this feat is possible because the tentacles are hollow.

Generally nocturnal, the snail seeks out the seclusion of the hedge bottom during the day, making its nightly rounds in search of food when dusk falls. Rain, particularly in the early evening, will tempt it out. It is perhaps extraordinary that an animal as lethargic-looking should trail back to the same sleeping quarters at the end of its excursions, and yet it does this with clockwork regularity, provided of course that it manages to escape the ravages of some hungry predator which can cope with its shell.

Breeding takes place during summer, when the snail will lay a number of batches of 40-100 eggs in holes in the ground. These virtually transparent round blobs, about one-eighth of an inch (3mm) in diameter, will hatch in about thirty days.

Slugs are also quite common in many hedges, the most noticeable, if not the most common, being the large or common black slug (*Arion ater*). The slug was probably named after examination of one particular specimen, for its colour varies widely: black, chocolate-brown and yellowish-brown are common. Perhaps even more than the snail, because its soft body is unprotected, the slug finds the seclusion of the hedge invaluable, especially when conditions are unfavourable.

The black slug can reach quite a size when fully grown and 8in (20cm) specimens are not uncommon; the average is around 4in (10cm). There are two pairs of tentacles, the largest having eyes at the tips.

Lacking any form of protection when touched, the slug contracts its body to form a mass; in this state it sways slowly from side to side, as if trying to hypnotise the onlooker, a characteristic peculiar to this species. For hibernation it seeks a hole in the ground.

The effect of hedgerow destruction on snails and slugs is not really known; indeed studies into the distribution of these molluscs is relatively recent. Some general inferences have resulted from them. Shelter has always been considered as one of the important factors which influences the distribution of terrestrial (land) snails and slugs. Arable regions are generally unfavourable, but hedges, ditches and roadside verges have traditionally alleviated the situation, and in many instances provided the most important habitats. The destruction of vast tracts of hedgerow, particularly in lowland England, where shelter and un-disturbed moist habitats are at a premium anyway, has almost certainly resulted in a decrease in the mollusc population—and a consequent decrease in food available for their many predators. They will have been affected by the increased use of herbicides, although it is known that contact poisons are not very effective in dealing with some molluscs, and slugs in particular resist them, because they tend to shed unwelcome chemicals in their mucus. Some research showed that slugs built up higher concentrations of DDT, when this was being used, than did some other invertebrates.

One of the commoner species of snails seeking out the shelter of the hedge is the brown-lipped or grove snail (*Cepaea nemoralis*). Some have actually been recorded at a height of 7ft (2m) above ground level, though generally they live at the bottom. One of the interesting features of the grove snail is the wide variety of shell colours and markings, which camouflage the snail in different habitats. Large numbers must nonetheless be discovered and eaten by thrushes, indicated by the litter of shells to be found in many hedge bottoms.

11
Hedgerow Crafts

Farmers' hedges did not grow up simply because a few bushes were planted. They have a specific function to perform, and must be managed in some way. The countryside craft of hedging and ditching evolved in response to a real need. Generations of care have been lavished on many thousands of miles of hedges; until the recent advent of fully mechanised low-labour farming methods, this management took a prominent place in the seasonal routine. Today, unfortunately, farmers or farm workers have too many jobs to do for hedge craftsmanship to be allowed much time. Furthermore, modern farming methods have meant that hedges are 'lost' land, when an increasing population demands more food.

Managing Hedges

Even today the craft of hedge management has not totally died. It is still carried out with a great deal of precision in parts of Northamptonshire, Lincolnshire and Leicestershire, to give specific instances. Hedge-laying became the traditional method of managing hedges, but unlike many rural crafts it was probably not widely practised until relatively recently in many areas, evolving to deal with the innumerable miles of hedges resulting from the Enclosure Acts and Awards of the eighteenth and nineteenth centuries. On a smaller scale it had been used for a very long time: Caesar described a typically laid hedge in his *Gallic War*.

Even though hedge-laying was never a universal form of hedge

No longer managed, the hedge is not stockproof and wire netting and stakes have been added (*D. F. Wright*)

maintenance, something had to be done to keep any hedge thick, stockproof and growing in the required line. One way of managing woodland in earlier times was to coppice it. Trees were cut down at regular intervals and from the stools or stumps an abundance of fresh shoots would spring out in all directions. In some districts hedges too were coppiced. Every ten to fifteen years or so, the complete hedge would have been chopped down to ground level. This method yielded useful wood for stakes and other purposes—hawthorn was used for firewood, other kinds were suitable for weaving into hurdles to pen in sheep. When coppicing was the locally established way of looking after hedges, it was probably necessary to have some form of rotation system. When the year to chop down the hedge came, it

Using traditional tools, this craftsman is attempting to lay a hedge in which shrubs have been allowed to grow for a long time without attention. Witness the size of some of the wood (*Leicester Mercury*)

would not have been possible to keep cattle in the field for several years, and so the land must have reverted to arable use.

Laying is the most efficient method of maintaining a stockproof hedge, although it is expensive in labour costs. Where hedges have been regularly laid, there is no need for any other form of barrier to keep stock inside; with other methods of management it is usually necessary to reinforce the hedge with hurdles or some form of wooden fencing. Not surprisingly it is in areas where stock farming predominates that hedge-laying has been most widely used.

An alternative to laying was known as brushing: the top and sides of the hedge would simply be trimmed at regular intervals, probably once annually. Until the recent use of mechanical cutters, this was probably the only means of managing hedges in certain areas. In some places brushing would be used as well as coppicing in order to stop hedges spreading over trackways. In some places, for instance parts of Lincolnshire, a line of barbed wire or sheep netting is sometimes placed about a yard away from the hedge to give additional stock-proofing.

Hedge laying is still of sufficient interest in certain areas for competition to be organised, such as those in Leicestershire run by the Hunt Hedge Cutting Societies. One of the fascinations of the national championships is that the competitors use different styles depending on the part of the country from which they come.

Hedge cutting and laying have always been winter activities, usually accompanied by the annual ditch-cleaning session. Other work on the land is slack then, and hedging has kept labourers busy as well as the hedges tidy. Also it is easier to cut and lay a hedge in winter, when most of the herbs have died down and the leaves have fallen from the trees and shrubs, giving a clear run for the craftsman. Hedging shrubs are allowed to grow to a height of 6 or 7ft (2m) before cutting and laying is carried out; then they need attention.

The traditional hedge layer works slowly and methodically, causing little enough disturbance to the wildlife of hedge, bank or ditch. The few tools he uses are of basically the same design all over the country, but there are some regional variations in shapes. He needs a long-handled slasher, a billhook and, where thick stems are a problem, an axe. He usually wears thick leather gloves, since the predominant hedgrow species, blackthorn and hawthorn—let alone brambles—are not noted for kindness to the skin. The true professional also covers his knees with thick pads, so that he can use them to push the stems into place.

Just as a wood carver has his own individual style and produces a unique piece of work, so the hedge layer will leave his inimitable stamp on his hedges. Nevertheless he will have a basic mode of attack, just as his ancestors have done for generations before him. He starts by removing weeds, undergrowth and dead wood from the bottom of the hedge, for over the year a great deal of rubbish, including blown leaves and dead plants, will have accumulated in the hedge bottoms. He then trims the sides of the hedge to remove surplus stems and any that have grown out of line, striking them off with deft upward

193

Using protective gloves, the hedger tidies up branches before laying them (*Leicester Mercury*)

A technique practised at least since the time of the Enclosures, and probably for centuries before that. This craftsman is interweaving the smaller, more pliable material in amongst the thicker branches, which have already been 'severed' and bent into position (*Leicester Mercury*)

strokes of his bill-hook to avoid splintering the wood, thus leaving a clean line. He also removes elder, bramble and any wood unsuitable for the hedge.

He is now ready for the actual laying. Most men work from left to right, and if the hedge is on a slope they often prefer to work up the gradient. Using his bill-hook, the hedge-layer chops through half the thickness of the first and subsequent stems, about half a metre from ground level. These he bends over individually at an angle of between 45° and 60°. The skill comes in only part-severing the branch: there must still be a link with the roots, so that the shrubs continue to obtain their nutrients in the following spring. At intervals of about 1½–2ft (45–60cm) he needs upright stakes around which he can weave his bent-over branches. If suitable saplings are growing where needed, then these can be trimmed to a height of 3ft (1m) or so, depending on the final height of the hedge. If no living post is available, a stake from elsewhere will be driven into the ground; its long-term durability is unimportant, since it will be removed in a few years when the hedge has established itself or is relaid.

The bent-over branches, known as *plashers*, are interwoven round the uprights, this process being known as plashing or pleaching. Each one is bent neatly to the same angle before being intertwined. In some areas hazel or elm rods are cut to size and woven in and out of the vertical posts to bind the top of the hedge, giving it a neat and finished appearance. These 'heathers' also help to hold down the newly woven branches, which could get out of place because of the natural springiness of hawthorn or blackthorn.

Where a hedge is well laid, the branches, especially at the bottom, will 'tiller out', shooting strongly, which helps to make the fence stockproof.

Where trees have been planted in the hedge, or have seeded themselves, they are often allowed to grow up to maturity at suitable intervals along the hedge. They will eventually form a valuable source of hardwood, and during their long lifetime they will provide much-needed shelter for livestock and act as windbreaks for crops.

When a hedge has reached maturity, the original shrubs will have become small trees. Certain rambling species like brambles, and wild

In some parts of the country, pieces of hedge are managed for a specific purpose. This is a horse jump at Everdon in Northamptonshire, where horse trials are held (*D. F. Wright*)

rose will be a nuisance if not cut back each year, as they spread into the roadside verge, decreasing its floral value as well as road visibility, and make inroads into the fields. Once the hedge has grown wild its function as a boundary is soon eroded. Usually, however, a neglected hedge can be relaid and restored.

The way in which a hedge is looked after is, as already mentioned, a key factor in its value as a wildlife habitat. In certain parts of the country hedges are managed for specific purposes, besides being barriers for fields. In fox-hunting country, for instance, hedges are kept neatly clipped and short to help the horses galloping full-tilt over the fields.

Hurdles and Hurdle Making

In sheep-farming country a great many hurdles were constantly required to construct temporary pens, dividing up fields to keep the sheep together and shelter them in bad weather or during lambing. This practice also served another useful purpose before the days of artificial fertilizer: sheep manure was of great importance for cereal crops.

It was part of the shepherd's daily chores to ensure that a new pen was ready for the sheep when the old one was 'finished'. Wattle hurdles were the easiest to make, and for a fold of a decent size a hundred or so were needed, usually made of hazelwood.

Ash is used for a different type of hurdle, the gate or bar hurdle, which resembles a six-bar gate.

As with other crafts hurdle-making has naturally died out in many areas, though hurdles sell readily enough where still obtainable. The hazel comes from coppiced woods, shoots which have been growing for about eight years being selected. As with hedging, coppicing was a winter task, the wood being removed when the sap was dormant. With changes in farming methods, wood is now cut at almost any time, although it is accepted that the hurdles made from summer wood will deteriorate much more quickly than those made of timber cut in the winter.

Both types of hurdle are made about 6ft by 3ft (2m by 1m), though dimensions vary slightly. The poles at the ends are longer so that the hurdles can be pushed into the ground—for which the help of a metal bar is needed in hard soil.

Where ash or hazel are scarce, the substitutes used include willow and chestnut, though these do not last as long. The pattern of the hurdle seems to have changed little over the centuries, and for speed of manufacture the design is simple.

The traditional hurdlemaker would start his task in winter and work in a clearing in the wood during some other part of the year, putting the hurdles together. It was usually a seasonal job, for the times he was not involved with other work on the farm.

His basic requirement is a hurdle mould. This is a slightly curved

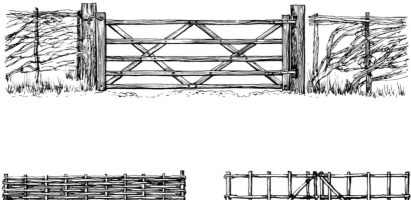

The traditional five-bar gate and two types of hurdle

piece of timber, about 7ft (2m) in length, drilled with ten holes. The thicker upright poles of the hurdle are pushed into these holes, the longer poles for pushing into the ground going at each end—these two are the 'shores'. The rest of the posts are known as sails. The wood for the body of the hurdle is then woven in and out of the uprights. As the worker reaches the end he gives the piece of wood a half twist, and then continues to weave again; by twisting the wood like this, the fibres will not be broken.

The process continues, new material being brought in as necessary until the desired height is reached. The hurdle is then removed from the mould, and tidied up ready for use. The curved mould of course results in a curved hurdle; then, when the hurdles have 'seasoned' as it were, they will straighten out and the fibres become taut. In shepherds' hurdles the craftsman will leave what is known as a 'twilly hole' so that they can be put on the pole and slung over a shoulder.

Gate hurdles are more open and do not offer the same degree of protection to the sheep, but they do act as windbreaks. The ash for the upright bars is usually taken from a tree sixteen to twenty-five years old. From the same tree the craftsman will usually select thicker rods for the uprights. Holes are made in these, in a kind of mortise joint. The centre of the gate hurdle has a further upright which adds strength, and there are also braces from the corners at the bottom to the centre of the top bar. The distance between each of the bars varies: the narrowest gap being at the bottom, the widest at the top. To prevent the wind from howling through in severe conditions, the shepherd will use straw bales.

Both types of hurdles are used for filling in gaps in hedges and other field boundaries, although the wattle type is usually the more effective.

Gates and Stiles

To the uninitiated a gate is a gate, but there are many variations in different parts of the country. The gate was once associated in people's minds with the Enclosure Acts, because all the newly enclosed fields needed gates, and most gateways do date from this time, from the eighteenth and nineteenth centuries, although of course there was some form of access to fields enclosed earlier.

The gates shown on old drawings and engravings are simple affairs. Hedge planting was a local undertaking, and the village carpenter would have been asked to provide the gates needed, making them to his own design which might become the norm for the area. Mass production and constant communication with other districts belonged to the future.

Early gates were usually a series of bars or poles which dropped into a slot; some form of 'retainer' would stop cattle from dislodging them. The modern gate shown on page 198 is similar to those of generations ago. Even two thousand years ago the Romans in Britain were using a gate, on the same lines as one or two primitive swinging gates still existing in remote corners such as on Dartmoor. Known as the wood and stone gate, one end of it was pivoted between two stones which formed part of a pillar or wall.

The basic structure of wooden field gates is much the same every-

A traditional five-barred gate across a green lane (*Goodman Photographics*)

where: each has two uprights, a top rail and a brace—a rail from the bottom on the hinge side to the middle of the top rail. Four rails below the top one are the most common, (the usual five-barred gate) though one more or less may be found. Local variations come in the additional bracing used—a double-X or some other arrangement of uprights to give more strength. The horizontal bars are usually spaced closer together near the bottom to deter small lambs from escaping. Many farm dogs can of course scramble up and over the bars.

Gate furniture—the latches, hinges and so forth—varies, though individual gate-making, like hurdle-making, is dying out. Metal gates are common in many areas even though they do not last indefinitely. Early in the 1800s a carpenter would have charged about 17s 6d. to 18s (90p) for making an oak farm gate 10ft (3m) across, taking about a day to complete it. Cleft oak, untreated, was most often used and if well made the gate might have lasted a hundred years. Later the wood was usually sawn, and recently softwood gates, which must be creosoted, have become common though they do not last long.

Where arable crops have replaced stock, the gate is of little consequence and a 'hosier' gate suffices—just three or four strands of barbed wire strung across a gap in the hedge.

Stiles can also present an interesting study: see those illustrated on page 37 for examples. In the days when people went from one place to another on foot, the quickest way was usually across country, and footpaths between hamlets, villages and isolated farms were important. To cut down costs and stop cattle escaping, stiles were placed where people needed to go·through the hedges. Footpaths with their stiles are again jealously guarded today, in many areas, if more for their amenity value to walkers than for strict utility.

Stiles vary greatly according to local traditions and materials. In Middlesex and Hertfordshire the V-shaped stile known as a squeezer was the local feature. The old rustic rail stile was common in other places. Essex had ladder stiles, and in some places the zigzag posts and kissing-gates featured widely.

In the eastern counties of England, and in a few other districts, the only barriers between one field and the next man's have been ditches. In other areas ditches were dug out to throw up a bank on which the hedge could be planted, at the time of the enclosures, their drainage function being a useful by-product. Although one of the regular jobs on many farms is ditching, the cost has greatly increased, along with that of maintaining hedges. Fields still need to be drained, but the initial heavy cost of installing underground pipes often proves more economical. So ditches in many places are being filled in or allowed to silt up; in other areas mechanical diggers are brought in to clear the channel.

12

The Garden Hedge

Even a garden hedge, properly managed and maintained, and containing suitable shrubs and tree species, can be a valuable nature reserve for wildlife. Although the plots may be small, if vast numbers of people planted and encouraged hedges round their gardens, some kind of replacement of the farmer's hedges would be available to wildlife.

A number of species of shrubs suitable for garden hedges will attract wildlife, and if trees can be planted in the hedge its value to plants and animals is greatly increased. Perhaps the most obvious beneficiaries are the birds, because we can watch them come and go. Of all the natural haunts in a garden it is to the hedge that the birds will look for shelter, not necessarily only when nest-building.

As with field hedges, hawthorn can easily be used; it grows fairly rapidly, and if managed properly provides a useful haunt for birds. Because it comes into leaf early it will naturally attract some of the earliest nesters, such as the blackbird. Blackthorn is also suitable for garden hedges. As with hawthorn the key to success is careful trimming, or as in a field hedge it can soon get out of hand.

Evergreen hedging is often wanted in a garden, and will offer some degree of shelter to bird visitors in hard weather. One of the most popular species recently is Leyland cypress (*Cupressocyparis leylandii*) and one of its greatest virtues is its speed of growth. It may reach a height of 10ft (3m) or more only six years after planting. Its evergreen leaves give off a distinctive, pleasant, scent. It does have at least one disadvantage: it is not totally hardy, and in severe winters might suffer.

For suburban gardens, the Leyland cypress is often considered as *the* hedge, but conifers are not everyone's choice.

Thirty or forty years ago, privet was the usual hedge shrub. Like the cypress it was probably planted because it is evergreen and a fast grower, and although the green variety seems to collect dust and often looks generally shabby, the golden form is extremely attractive. Properly trimmed and well maintained it provides a good hedge and offers nesting sites for many birds. It is hardy and can be grown readily from cuttings in most areas. The disadvantage is that the roots spread, preventing other plants from growing and taking much from the soil. A hedge of the green and gold varieties together can be striking. The golden variety grows rather more slowly than the green form, but it is possible to overcome this by trimming back the green species at shorter intervals. Another useful way to plant privet is as two hedges, with a distance of 2–3ft (0.8–1m) between the two.

Although as a tree the beech (*Fagus sylvatica*) is a deciduous species, losing its leaves in autumn, as a hedge it retains much of its foliage throughout the winter, the old muddy-brown leaves only falling as the new ones appear. It has been used successfully as a hedging species for many years. It tolerates most soil conditions, except where the ground is heavy and wet and produces a very thick hedge, which makes an effective windbreak in the garden. Its one great drawback is that it grows very slowly; even in good conditions it is hardly likely to have reached 4ft or so (1.2m) within six years, so it is many years before it becomes thick and tall enough to attract nesting birds.

Holly is recommended by many authorities for hedging, but it is a slow grower. The berries could ultimately provide a very useful supply of food for birds in the winter: 'could' is the operative word, since male and female trees are needed, to allow cross-pollination. Once established it provides the garden with an effective windbreak—and keeps out the neighbours' cats and dogs

In some areas hornbeam has long been used for hedges. As with beech, the leaves tend to hang on the twigs much longer than with many other deciduous species. It grows reasonably quickly and within six years a hedge 7ft (2m) or so can be expected in good soils. Unlike many other species it grows out about 3ft (1m) at the base, and so needs more space than a small garden can usually spare.

Some of the decorative shrub-like species are often grown as hedges. These include Chinese honeysuckle, berberis and pyracantha. Pyracantha grows very quickly, and depending on the species has orange, red or yellow berries. Although it grows well, it is only at its best in a sunny situation. The berries provide a good supply of food for birds in the autumn and for a reasonable crop to be produced care must be taken not to clip the shrub too close.

Although Chinese honeysuckle provides a good hedge, once established, and its small flowers are attractive in the garden, it does have drawbacks: not least of these is that if it is allowed to grow more than 3ft (1m) or so in height it tends to break open in the centre, becoming particularly prone to collapse under any weight of snow.

A number of species of berberis are suitable for hedges. As an evergreen, berberis has its advantages, providing shelter for birds and to some extent other animals, including small mammals in severe conditions. Once established it forms a sturdy barrier and an effective windbreak. It grows quite quickly, but needs to be allowed to attain a width of about 7ft (2m) around the base.

Index

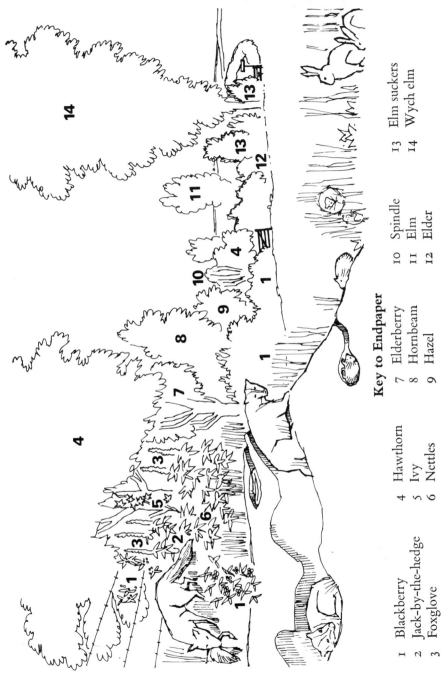

Key to Endpaper

1	Blackberry	4	Hawthorn	7	Elderberry	10 Spindle
2	Jack-by-the-hedge	5	Ivy	8	Hornbeam	11 Elm
3	Foxglove	6	Nettles	9	Hazel	12 Elder

13 Elm suckers
14 Wych elm